Black Holes

and Other Works of God

God Seen. Everything Changes.

MICHAEL D. GRAYSON

MGM PARTNERS LTD.

Copyright

Black Holes and Other Works of God

God Seen. Everything Changes.

Updated: July 2026

Second Edition

ISBN (Paperback): 978-0-9817775-5-9
ISBN (eBook): 978-0-9817775-6-6
ISBN (Audio Book): 978-0-9817775-4-2

Library of Congress Number: 2025948150

Edited by Pamela K. Grayson

Cover design by Michael D. Grayson with Image Creator AI

Published by MGM Partners Ltd.

Printed in the United States of America

Distributed by Amazon KDP and IngramSpark

Website: MGMPartnersPublishing.com

Dedication

To Pam,

My wife, my closest friend, and the one who has walked every step of this journey with me.

Thank you for your unwavering love, your steadfast encouragement, and the quiet strength you have shown through years of deep conversations, endless revisions, and the shared wonder of discovering God's glory in both Scripture and the cosmos.

This book exists because of your partnership, your prayers, and your belief in its message.

With all my love,

Mike

Table of Contents

The Journey Begins Here

People want to believe they are in control.

That they can think clearly, make good decisions, and navigate life on their own terms. There is a certain confidence in that—the idea of being the captain of your own ship, the master of your own future.

And for a time, that confidence can feel justified.

But it doesn't last.

Because sooner or later, life pushes back.

The plans you carefully put in place begin to unravel. Circumstances shift without warning. A door closes that you thought would always be open. A relationship you depended on changes—or disappears entirely. What once felt stable begins to move beneath your feet.

And when that happens, something becomes very clear:

You are not in control.

At that point, the question is no longer theoretical. It

becomes deeply personal.

What do you do when your plans fall apart?
What do you do when you cannot fix it?

Those are not abstract questions. At some point, they become all too real.

You reach a place where your plans are no longer working, where the outcome is uncertain, and where the weight of it all begins to settle in. And in that moment, you do what most of us eventually do—you turn to God. You ask Him for help. You ask Him to intervene, to give you clarity, to carry you through something you know you cannot carry on your own.

And that is exactly where Scripture meets you.

The Apostle James speaks from experience. He speaks into that moment and says something that almost feels out of place at first: *"Consider it all joy... when you encounter various trials."* Not because the trial itself is pleasant, but because something is happening in you through it. The trial tests your faith and that testing is producing endurance. And if you allow that process to run its course, it leads somewhere—it leads to a kind of steadiness, a completeness, a life that is no longer fragile and easily shaken.

But then James moves from what God is doing *through* the trial to what you are to do *in* the trial.

"If any of you lacks wisdom, let him ask of God..."

And you do ask.

You ask because you need direction. You ask because you don't know what to do next. You ask because you are standing in the middle of something that is bigger than you.

But James does not stop there. He adds something that reaches deeper than the request itself:

"But he must ask in faith without any doubting..."

Now the focus shifts.

It is no longer about your situation. It is about what you believe about God.

Because the one who doubts is described as being like the surf of the sea—driven and tossed by the wind. That picture is not hard to recognize. It is the back-and-forth that happens inside of you. One moment you are confident that God will carry you through, and the next moment you are questioning whether anything will change at all. You move between trust and uncertainty, never quite settling, never quite at rest.

And James explains why.

It is not simply that life is unstable. It is that the heart is divided.

You are asking God for help, but at the same time, you are not entirely convinced that He is able to give it. You are reaching toward Him, but you are still holding on to the idea that everything ultimately depends on you.

And that tension leaves you unsettled.

So, the real issue is not whether you will ask God for help. The real issue is whether you believe that He is who He says He is—whether you believe that He has the power, the authority, and the willingness to act in your life.

Because if you are unsure about that, then of course you will feel like you are being tossed back and forth. You are trying to stand on something you have not yet fully seen.

And that is the heart of this book.

It is written to help you see God clearly—not as an idea, not as a distant figure, but as the Creator who spoke light into existence and established the very laws that govern everything you experience. Because when you begin to see Him as He truly is, the question of whether He is able begins to fade, and the instability that once defined your thinking begins to give way to something solid.

That raises a deeper issue worth exploring:

What does it really mean to see God clearly?

Because if your confidence in Him is going to hold—especially in the middle of trials—it cannot rest on vague ideas or secondhand assumptions. It has to be grounded in something real. Something that shows you not only that God exists, but that He is powerful, present, and fully capable of acting in your life.

Scripture does not leave that unanswered.

It takes you back to the beginning.

To the moment where everything began.

"Let there be light."

Those words are not just familiar—they are foundational. They are not poetic language meant to inspire; they are a declaration of power. In a single command, God brings into existence something that had never existed before. Not by effort. Not by process. But by His word.

That moment tells you something essential about who He is.

He is not limited. He is not constrained. He is not working within a system—He is the One who created it.

And that is where your understanding begins to expand.

Because the more closely you examine the world that came from that command—the structure of reality, the consistency of its laws, the boundaries that even the most extreme environments cannot break—the more clearly you begin to see that creation is not random.

It is governed.

It is precise.

It is held together by something far greater than chance.

And that includes everything from the light that fills the universe... to the places where even light cannot escape.

Places like black holes.

There, gravity is so powerful that light itself cannot escape. Time stretches toward infinity near the event horizon. Yet even at these outer limits of reality, the universe does not collapse into chaos. It displays order, boundaries, and mathematical exactness that refuse to behave like an accident.

Over twenty years of studying both quantum physics and Scripture, I discovered something profound: the physical universe and the biblical account are not in conflict. They reveal a remarkable continuity.

The God who said "Let there be light" is the same One whose fingerprints appear in the structure of energy, the behavior of matter, the bending of spacetime, and the silent power of black holes. This is not abstract theory. It is evidence of a governed creation—lawful, intelligible, and intentionally designed.

Why does this matter to *you*?

Because how you understand the universe shapes how you understand everything else—including yourself.

If the cosmos is random and accidental, then meaning, morality, and purpose become whatever we decide in the moment. Identity becomes self-invented. Security feels fragile because nothing is truly fixed.

But if the universe is a coherent creation sustained by the same God who spoke it into being, then reality itself has an Author. Standards are not invented—they are discovered. Dignity is inherent, not assigned. Purpose is built in, not negotiated. And the One who set the unbreakable speed of light and the limits of spacetime is powerful enough to bring order to your life as well.

This book is written to help you see that truth clearly—and to let it change how you live—to help you find your purpose.

In Part One, "God Seen. Everything Changes," we explore the personal transformation that occurs when you truly recognize God as Creator and King.

Drawing from the stories of John Newton, the wonder of Psalm 8, and the sweeping kingdom narrative of Scripture, you'll discover how seeing God rightly reorients your identity, your sense of security, your understanding of right and wrong, and your confidence in the future.

When God is no longer distant or optional but visible in the majesty of His works, anxiety loses its grip and purpose comes into focus.

In Part Two, we turn to the science with honest curiosity and accessible explanation. You will learn how energy forms the building block of all creation, how light and matter are intimately connected, how Einstein's relativity reveals the structure of space and time, and how my proposed Theory of Universal Motion traces conserved order from the smallest quantum scales to the largest cosmic structures.

We'll examine black holes not as mysteries that undermine faith, but as powerful reminders of the boundaries and coherence built into reality.

You'll see how even the most extreme phenomena point back to a Creator whose power and wisdom far exceed our own.

The result is practical and hopefully life changing.

You will gain a stronger foundation for your faith—one that stands up to questions, doubts, and the challenges of a secular world.

You will develop a clearer worldview that equips you to navigate moral confusion, identity struggles, and cultural chaos with confidence.

Most importantly, you will encounter the God who is not threatened by science but revealed through it—the same God who offers you forgiveness, purpose, and eternal security through Jesus Christ.

You do not need a degree in physics or theology to benefit from these pages. You only need an open heart and a willingness to look again at the world around you.

Because when you truly see the God who spoke light into existence—and who still sustains every law that governs galaxies and black holes—your view of reality, of yourself, and of your future cannot remain the same.

Everything changes.

And that change brings the security, clarity, and peace you have been longing for.

Welcome to *Black Holes and Other Works of God.*

Part 1

God Seen. Everything Changes.

1 — The Moment Everything Changes

"When I consider Your heavens, the work of Your fingers, The moon and the stars, which You have ordained; What is man that You take thought of him, And the son of man that You care for him? Yet You have made him a little lower than God, And You crown him with glory and majesty!"

Psalm 8:3-5 NASB

Before he wrote the song Amazing Grace, John Newton was not confused about who was in charge of his life.

He was.

Born in 1725, he went to sea as a teenager. By his early twenties, he was immersed in the Atlantic slave trade. He transported human beings in chains across the ocean. He drank heavily. He mocked faith openly. He rejected moral restraint. He prided himself on being hardened.

He did not consider himself evil.

He considered himself realistic.

Life was survival. Power. Opportunity. Profit.
Religion was weakness.

One night in 1748, his ship was caught in a violent storm in the North Atlantic. The vessel groaned under the force of wind and water. The crew expected death. Newton, who had mocked God for years, found himself doing something he had not done sincerely in a long time.

He prayed.
Not eloquently.
Not theologically.
Just desperately.
"Lord, have mercy on us."

The storm did not instantly calm. The ship did not immediately stabilize. But something shifted.

For the first time, Newton recognized that he was not the final authority. He was not in control. He was not self-sufficient. He was not sovereign.

That moment did not make him instantly righteous. It did not immediately reform his profession. But it cracked the illusion.

He later described it as the beginning of his awakening.

Over time, he left the slave trade. He became a pastor. And eventually he wrote the words that have outlived empires:

"Amazing grace, how sweet the sound,
That saved a wretch like me.
I once was lost,
but now am found,
Was blind, but now I see."

Notice the language.

Lost.
Blind.
Found.
See.

Newton did not describe his former life primarily as immoral. He described it as blind.

His blindness wasn't the inability to see; it was a lack of awareness.

When he "saw"—everything changed.

Not because circumstances improved. But because authority shifted.

He no longer saw himself as self-governing. He saw himself as accountable. Dependent. Known.

The man who once trafficked in human misery became a voice against it.

The same mind.
The same personality.
The same abilities.
But a different authority.

Freedom and Authority

John Newton's storm did more than change the direction of his life.

It exposed something deeper—something that reaches far beyond a single moment at sea. It revealed how easily we assume control, how naturally we place ourselves at the center, and how quickly that illusion breaks when life pushes back.

But that same question—*Who is really in charge?*—does not only surface in moments of crisis.

It shows up in how we think about everything.

A person who says, "I answer only to myself," is still living under something—desire, pride, anger, appetite, fear, status, pleasure, resentment, or power. Jesus said, "Everyone who practices sin is a slave to sin" (John 8:34). Self-rule often looks like freedom at first, but it eventually becomes another master.

Today, we live in a world that is deeply confident in its ability to explain itself. Science has given us extraordinary insight into the workings of the universe. We can measure, predict, and model with remarkable precision. And because of that, many have come to believe that the need for God has been replaced—or at the very least, reduced.

Not rejected outright in every case, but quietly set aside.

For some, God is no longer necessary.

For others, He is distant—unrelated to the real world of

cause and effect.

And for many, the question is no longer *"Who is my authority?"* but *"Do I need one at all?"*

They may feel free, but Scripture says they are not. They have not escaped authority; they have made the self their authority. That is the oldest temptation: "You will be like God" (Genesis 3:5).

Because removing God from our understanding of the world does not eliminate authority—it simply replaces it.

The issue is no longer just what happened to John Newton in a storm. It concerns what we believe about the world we inhabit every day.

Science Reveals God

And that brings us to another Newton.

A hundred years earlier, Isaac Newton was also wrestling with authority—not of the sea, but with the laws of the physical world around him.

Sir Isaac Newton was known on more than one occasion to sign his work with the autograph in Latin, "*Numero pondere et mensura Deus omnia condidit*", which translated means *"God created everything by number, weight and measure".*[1]

That statement reflects a perspective that is not

---

[1] Today in Science History. *Sir Isaac Newton Quotes on God.*https://todayinsci.com/N/Newton_Isaac/NewtonIsaac-God-Quotations.htm

universally accepted.

For some, the idea that science points to God is unacceptable. If science is to remain “objective,” then God must be removed from the conversation entirely.

Others respond differently. They see the same laws, the same precision, the same order—and conclude that these are not arguments against God, but evidence of design.

What changes is not what we see, but how we understand what we are seeing. And that raises a quiet question—why is it that the same world can lead one person to dismiss God, and another to see His hand in everything?

That question matters more than it may seem.

Because the difference is not just in what we conclude—it shapes how we live. It shapes what we trust, what we value, and how we understand our place in the world.

If the same creation can lead one person to dismiss God and another to see His hand in everything, then the issue is not simply what we see.

It is how we are seeing it.

And that is where this journey begins.

It begins with a simple but foundational premise:

God is the Source—the Creator.

To explore the universe while excluding its Source is not a small decision. It is to accept only part of the picture, while leaving out the very thing that gives it meaning.

Why This Matters

At first glance, the debate between science and faith may seem abstract—something confined to universities, laboratories, or online arguments. But the question of whether there is a Creator behind the cosmos is not merely academic.

It is deeply personal.

If there is no Creator, then you are the product of blind forces. Your existence is the outcome of chemical accidents stretched across billions of years. Meaning becomes self-defined. Morality becomes negotiated. Purpose becomes optional.

But if there is a Creator—if the universe was spoken into existence by intention rather than assembled by accident—then your life is not random. You were not merely formed by energy—you were formed with purpose.

The question of God determines how you understand yourself—

whether dignity is inherent or assigned,
whether right and wrong are relative,
whether life has meaning or is an illusion.

When you look at the night sky and feel small, that feeling can lead in two directions. It can lead to insignificance. Or it can lead to wonder.

At the beginning of this chapter, I quoted Psalm 8. It

does not deny our smallness. It acknowledges it. Yet in the same breath it declares that we are *crowned with glory and majesty*. That paradox only makes sense if there is a Creator who both designed the cosmos and knows your name.

This is why the question of whether or not God exists cannot be avoided.

Because how you answer it shapes how you live—and who you are.

And it shapes what science itself becomes.

The Central Issue

It is not merely whether God exists.

The real issue is this:
Who is your authority?

John Newton thought he was.
Until he saw.
When he saw,
everything changed.

When God is seen clearly, everything changes—not only how we understand the universe, but how we understand ourselves within it.

If light, law, and boundaries reveal a Mind behind creation, then creation must have intention. And if it has intention, then it has direction.

Which brings us to the next question.

Not merely—*Who is your authority?*

But—

Why did He create the universe and mankind?

2 — God's Purpose for Creation

"then the dust will return to the earth as it was,
and the spirit will return to God who gave it."

Ecclesiastes 12:7

What is God's purpose?

God is not hidden behind creation. He has spoken through every physical law, every boundary, and every beautiful pattern. Nothing is accidental.

If God is the Creator, then the cosmos is far more than random events or cosmic coincidence. It is an intentional act. And every intentional act flows from purpose.

This makes the question deeply personal:

What is God saying about why we are here?

Cause and Effect—Time and Eternity

Isaac Newton famously observed that every action produces a corresponding reaction. At the deepest level, the universe itself reflects this larger principle. We often refer to it as "cause and effect".

If you walk along a deserted beach and see a fresh footprint in the sand, you do not assume the sand arranged itself that way. You conclude someone stepped there. The footprint began to exist—therefore, something caused it.

Why is this important to you?

Because for the universe to exist, there must be a cause. Something cannot come from nothing. And since you are part of the universe, you have a vested interest in its origin.

Consider the First Law of Thermodynamics—energy cannot be created or destroyed; it can only change forms.

That law of physics has very dramatic implications.

- All the energy in the universe had to come from a source outside itself.
- All of the energy in the universe today has existed from the beginning.
- Our universe is contained so that none of the energy is either lost or added to. One might think of the universe as a giant snow globe.

If the universe and its energy had a beginning, then the source of that beginning must lie beyond the physical system itself.[2]

Theoretical physicist Stephen Hawking acknowledged the difficulty of explaining a beginning without something beyond the universe when he wrote:

> *"In an unchanging universe, a beginning in time is something that has to be imposed by some being outside the universe."*[3]

That conclusion points toward the necessity of a cause beyond space, time, matter, and energy itself. Scripture identifies that cause as God—the eternal Creator who spoke all things into existence.

Understanding Eternity

Eternity is so vast that most people throw up their hands and say, "Nobody can really understand that." And they're right. We cannot fully comprehend eternity any more than a goldfish can comprehend the ocean.

But we can glimpse it.

Imagine the past, present, and future lined up on a single timeline.

Got that image in your mind?

Now ask yourself: **How big is the future?**

According to Scripture, the future stretches into

---

[2] Boles, Michael & Cengel, Yunus. "Thermodynamics: An Engineering Approach, 9th Edition". McGraw Hill 2019

[3] Hawking, Stephen. A Brief History of Time (p. 9). Random House Publishing Group. (April 1988)

eternity—limitless and unending.

How big is the past?

From our perspective, it stretches back to the beginning of the universe—however far that may be. To us, it feels unimaginably vast.

Both the past and the future are effectively infinite *from our limited human viewpoint.*

Now comes the most important question:

How big is the present?

Pause for a moment and think about it.

The instant you speak a word, that moment is already gone—pushed into the past.

By the time you become aware of a thought, that moment has already slipped away.

So how large is the present?

It is infinitely small.

The present exists, yet it is so fleeting we cannot grasp or hold it. We stand balanced on a razor-thin line between two infinities: an immeasurable past behind us and an immeasurable future ahead of us. Our entire lives are lived on a point so small it cannot even be measured.

Here is the striking implication:

If something as infinitely small as the present can exist,

why is it so difficult to believe that Someone infinitely *greater* than time can exist?

Perhaps the greatest limitation is not that God is beyond reality—but that *we* are trapped inside only a tiny slice of it.

God does not merely pass through time.

He transcends it.

He is Eternal.

And if God truly exists beyond time itself, then creation is not merely an event buried somewhere in the distant past. It is the moment the Author of eternity spoke the universe into existence.

This naturally prompts a deeper consideration:

What would we expect to see if an eternal God created a physical universe?

For centuries, people assumed science and Scripture stood in opposition. Yet the deeper we peer into the structure of reality, the more fascinating the opening words of Genesis become.

Bridging Science and Scripture

> *"The earth was formless and void, and darkness was over the surface of the deep, and the Spirit of God was moving over the surface of the waters. Then God said, "Let there be light"; and there was light."*
>
> *Genesis 1:2-3 NASB*

Some may question how the Genesis account aligns with modern physics. A literal interpretation need not conflict with scientific discovery; instead, it can complement it. Genesis 1:3 states, 'Then God said, "Let there be light"; and there was light.'

This command to create light aligns with modern cosmology, where light (photons) and energy form the foundation of all matter.

Faith and science are partners in revealing the Creator's glory—sometimes in the most unexpected places, like the spark that begins every human life.

The Spark of Life: Where Science meets Creation

Our universe began with a flash of light (Gen 1:3).

You too began with a flash of light.[4] Scientists at Northwestern University captured this moment on film: at the instant a human sperm fertilizes an egg, a brilliant burst of zinc sparks erupts.[5] The light explodes for about 20

[4] Bernhardt, M. L., Kim, A. M., O'Halloran, T. V. & Woodruff, T. K. "Zinc requirement during meiosis I-meiosis II transition in mouse oocytes is independent of the MOS-MAPK pathway". Biol Reprod 84, 526–536 (2011).

[5] Krauchunas, A. R. & Wolfner, M. F. Molecular changes during egg

seconds, then gradually fades over the next minute. In that brief window, two half-cells (meiotic) merge into one complete cell (mitotic) with a unique full set of DNA—creating a new human being distinct from both parents.

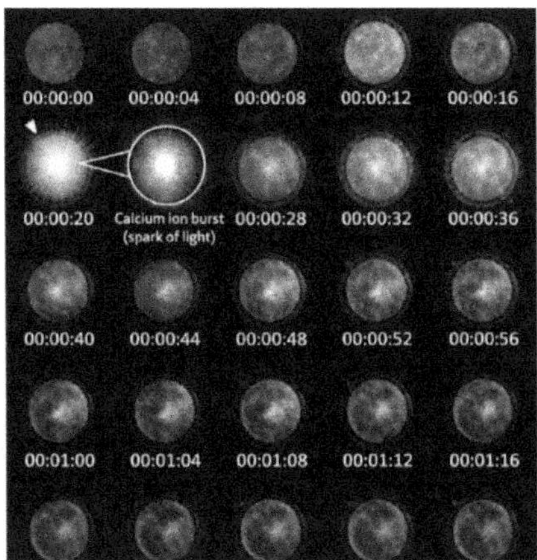

The brilliant spark that begins every human life mirrors the light that birthed the cosmos. Yet neither exists in a vacuum.

To understand their shared purpose, we must step back and see the larger stage: not just one physical universe, but two intertwined realms—Heaven and Earth.

The Two Realms: Heaven and Earth

That brilliant spark at the beginning of every human life does not happen in isolation. If both the universe and each person begin with purposeful light, they must belong to a larger story—one that existed long before our physical world.

---

activation. Current topics in developmental biology 102, 267–292 (2013).

Our expanding universe naturally raises big questions: What is it expanding into? Is there only one universe? Scripture gives us the answer by revealing two distinct realms: the material universe we inhabit and the eternal Kingdom of Heaven that preceded it.

Before the physical cosmos came into being, God existed eternally, outside of time and space.

"Before the mountains were born or You gave birth to the earth and the world, even from everlasting to everlasting, You are God." (Psalm 90:2 NASB)

"In the beginning was the Word, and the Word was with God, and the Word was God. He was in the beginning with God. All things came into being through Him..." (John 1:1-3 NASB)

"In the beginning God created the heavens and the earth." (Genesis 1:1 NASB)

These verses show that God's heavenly realm is not part of the created universe—it transcends it.

Jesus reinforced this dual reality throughout His teaching. Made in God's image, human beings are uniquely designed to bridge both realms: we live as physical creatures on Earth while carrying a spiritual awareness of Heaven.

This is why Jesus taught His disciples to pray:

"Our Father in heaven, hallowed be Your name.
Your ***kingdom*** *come.*
Your will be done, on earth as it is in heaven...

For Yours is the ***kingdom*** *and the power and the glory forever. Amen."*

(Matthew 6:9-13 NASB)

Notice how the Lord's Prayer—known by heart to millions—both begins and ends with the Kingdom.

Jesus placed the Kingdom at the very center of prayer because it is at the center of God's plan. The prayer is not just a request for daily bread or protection; it is a declaration that Heaven's reality should break into Earth's story.

This dual reality sets the stage for the central drama of Scripture: a cosmic conflict over who has the right to rule.

Why Did God Create this Universe?

If creation has purpose, then we must ask the deeper question: Why did God create this universe at all?

Many believers would answer that the Bible's central theme is the salvation of mankind. That is true—but only partly so. The Bible's overarching theme is **the restoration of God's Kingdom** in the face of rebellion.

Before this world existed, perfect peace and unity filled God's eternal Kingdom. Angels worshipped and served Him without conflict.

Yet one powerful angelic being, described as perfect in beauty and wisdom, used the freedom of choice God had given him and allowed pride to rise in his heart. He sought to usurp God's throne and establish his own rule (Isaiah 14:12-14; Ezekiel 28:12-15).

Other angels joined him in this rebellion. This act fractured the heavenly realm and introduced a false kingdom in opposition to God's rightful authority.

Because the angels exercised their God-given ability to choose, their decision was final. Fallen angels remain under judgment with no plan of redemption. In contrast, God created humanity with both the freedom to choose and the extraordinary offer of redemption through faith in Christ.

As a result, God created the heavens and the earth—a new stage where the question of sovereignty would be settled. Earth became the battleground. Satan and his followers were cast down here (Revelation 12:7-9), and humanity was introduced as a new order of beings made in God's own image.

We were commissioned to rule over the earth as God's representatives:

"Then God said, 'Let Us make man in Our image, according to Our likeness; and let them rule...'" (Genesis 1:26 NASB)"

Yet You have made him a little lower than God, and You crown him with glory and majesty! You make him to rule over the works of Your hands..." (Psalm 8:5-6 NASB)

But we know the story: humanity joined the rebellion through Adam's fall. The rightful rule God intended for us was lost—until Jesus, the perfect God-man, succeeded where mankind had failed.

This is why Jesus began His public ministry proclaiming

the Kingdom of God and taught us to pray, "Your kingdom come."

The Lord's Prayer is not a side note; it is a direct echo of the Bible's central plot line. God is restoring what was broken.

The conflict will reach its climax when Satan's false kingdom is fully defeated. The covenants will be fulfilled, the earth renewed, and God's eternal Kingdom established without rival.

"Then I saw a new heaven and a new earth..." (Revelation 21:1)

At that day, "every knee will bow... and every tongue will confess that Jesus Christ is Lord, to the glory of God the Father" (Philippians 2:9-11 NASB).

The same God who said "Let there be light" at the dawn of creation is guiding history toward this glorious restoration.

The spark that began the universe and the spark that begins each human life are not random. They are invitations—calling us to align our lives with the Kingdom that will ultimately prevail. This is the story we are living in. This is why we were created.

Finding Clarity in a Confusing World

In a world that often feels noisy and uncertain, it's easy to wonder why so many people struggle to see the clear, beautiful purpose we've been talking about.

Many today have grown up hearing that the universe is an accident, that Scripture can't be trusted, or that God is distant and uninvolved. Secular voices dismiss the covenants that reveal God's loving plan to restore and bless the whole earth.

Yet none of this surprises our Father. He knows the confusion, and He has never left us without light.

Even in the midst of skepticism, God's truth still shines. He reminds us:

> *"For My thoughts are not your thoughts, nor are your ways My ways," declares the Lord. "For as the heavens are higher than the earth, so are My ways higher than your ways and My thoughts than your thoughts." (Isaiah 55:8-9)*

The same God who made the covenants with Abraham and promised a New Covenant of forgiveness is still faithfully working to bless all nations and restore what was broken. His plans have not failed — they are unfolding, right on schedule.

Yes, there is an enemy who loves to stir up confusion. Satan's ancient rebellion continues as he tries to blind eyes and twist truth (2 Corinthians 4:4; Revelation 12:9). But his power is limited, and his defeat is certain. He cannot stop the light that broke into the universe, the light that sparkles at the beginning of every new life, or the greater Light who is Jesus Christ.

That is why Scripture gives us such tender, hope-filled invitations:

> *"Trust in the Lord with all your heart, and do not lean on your own understanding. In all your ways acknowledge Him, and He will make your paths straight." (Proverbs 3:5-6)*
>
> *"But seek first His kingdom and His righteousness, and all these things will be provided to you." (Matthew 6:33)*
>
> *"Jesus said to him, 'I am the way, and the truth, and the life; no one comes to the Father except through Me.'" (John 14:6)*

Clarity is not something we have to manufacture. It comes as a gift when we simply turn our hearts toward the One who spoke light into darkness.

The same Creator who formed the mountains, filled the oceans, and kindled the spark of life in you is patiently waiting to reveal more of Himself. The more we open our eyes to His creation and open our hearts to His Word, the more the fog lifts and the beauty of His Kingdom comes into focus.

You don't have to have all the answers today. You only need a willing heart. And that is something our gracious Father delights to meet with open arms.

Knowing God Through His Creation

In Genesis, quantum energy was transformed into increasingly complex forms of atoms and molecules until human life was created.

From the Christian perspective, comprehending quantum energy becomes pivotal in understanding our universe and the divine hand behind it all.

There is an indisputable truth about God's existence. Why do I say the truth of God's existence is indisputable?

Because the mere act of looking at the majesty of great mountains, vast oceans, and towering redwoods attest to His existence.

All we have to do is open our eyes and see the world that surrounds us. The sky and the trees, the sun and the stars, the ocean and the land, all declare His existence.

This is called God's "natural revelation" because He reveals Himself through nature. God has taken the first step in establishing a relationship with us by revealing Himself through His creation, and we must take the next step in recognizing Him as the Creator.

You Have a Purpose

In this chapter we have begun to follow the evidence of design—from the first light of creation to the spark of light at conception, from the reality of heaven and earth to the conflict of kingdoms that explains the moral tension of history.

The universe is not only *made*—it has *meaning*.

God's design does more than prove His existence. It reveals His intention.

And that intention is not vague. Scripture presents a unified story.

God's kingdom is real, His sovereignty is rightful, and His purpose is to restore what rebellion fractured.

That is why confusion is so dangerous—it does not merely distort ideas; it obscures the very plan that gives life meaning.

The answer to confusion is not cynicism—it is an open mind.

If creation is designed, then you are not lost in it. You are placed within it—called to see, to understand, and to seek the King whose world this is.

You Were Not an Afterthought

Look at the arc of what we have seen.

Light bursts into existence at the dawn of the universe.
Light flashes at the beginning of human life.
Heaven precedes earth.
A kingdom precedes history.
A conflict precedes your birth.

You did not enter a random world.

You entered a story already in motion.

Before you ever drew breath, a question was already echoing through creation:

Who has the right to rule?

Satan challenged it.
Angels chose sides.

Earth became the arena.
Humanity was given the power of allegiance.

And then you were born.

Not as an accident of chemistry.
Not as an unintended byproduct of energy.
But as an image-bearer placed inside a kingdom conflict with the capacity to choose.

This is why creation matters.

If the universe is intentional, then you are intentional.
If the kingdom is real, then your life has context.
If Christ will ultimately reign, then history is not accidental—it is unfolding.

Confusion clouds this truth. Culture distorts it. Skepticism questions it.

But the structure of reality still stands.

The heavens declare.
The cell ignites.
The covenants unfold.
The King reigns.

You are not drifting through meaningless space.

You are living inside a deliberate design.

And design always implies purpose.

We are no longer simply asking whether God created.

The deeper issue becomes:

Will you keep an open mind and examine the kingdom you are already standing in?

Because when you see that creation is purposeful, you begin to see that you are, too.

And that realization changes your worldview and how you live.

Chapter 2: Summary

This chapter begins with a simple but profound question—Why did God create at all?—and leads us on a journey from the wonders of creation to the heart of His eternal purpose.

We saw that the universe is not an accident. From the cause behind its beginning, to the razor-thin present caught between two infinities, to the brilliant flash of light at the dawn of creation and at the spark of every human life, everything bears the mark of intentional design. Faith and science join hands in declaring the glory of the Creator.

Scripture reveals the bigger story: before our physical world existed, God reigned in perfect peace in His eternal Kingdom. Rebellion fractured that peace, and this earth became the stage where the question of rightful rule would be answered. Humanity was lovingly placed in the middle of that story—not as bystanders, but as image-bearers with the freedom to choose allegiance and the breathtaking invitation to join God in restoring what was broken.

Even when confusion clouds our vision, God's truth still shines. He patiently calls us to trust Him, seek His Kingdom first, and fix our eyes on Jesus—the One who is the Way, the Truth, and the Life.

You were never an afterthought.

You were born into a purposeful universe, inside a meaningful story, with a real part to play in God's unfolding Kingdom. If creation is intentional, then so are you.

And that truth has the power to change how you see everything.

3 — Authority

"For although they knew God, they did not glorify him as God or give him thanks, but they became futile in their thoughts and their senseless hearts were darkened."

Romans 1:21 NET

Legislating Morality

Every society legislates morality. Every law ever written declares that one behavior is right and another is wrong. Laws against murder, theft, fraud, assault, and perjury are all moral judgments. Even those who insist that morality should never be legislated unknowingly rely on moral laws every day, because the moment we prohibit one action or protect another, we have declared that one choice is better than the other.

The real question, then, is not whether morality should shape society. It always does. The deeper question is far more important:

Whose morality will it be?

History offers sobering answers.

In the early 1930s, a farming family in Ukraine lived much as families had for generations. They worked from sunrise until sunset, tended their fields, cared for their livestock, and dreamed of passing the farm on to their children. Their labor was honest, and their harvest represented years of sacrifice and perseverance. They believed that providing for their family was both a responsibility and a virtue.

Then everything changed—not because the land stopped producing, but because the government redefined what was considered good and evil.

Private ownership was declared immoral. Keeping the grain they had grown was labeled selfish. Families who had once been admired for their hard work were suddenly condemned as enemies of the people. Soldiers arrived without warning, confiscating crops, livestock, tools, and even seed that had been set aside for the following year's planting. Fathers disappeared into labor camps. Mothers watched helplessly as their children grew weak from starvation. Millions would eventually perish in what history remembers as the Holodomor, not because nature had failed them, but because a government had replaced one moral standard with another.

Only one thing had changed.

Someone else now claimed the authority to define right

and wrong.

A generation later and half a world away, another family experienced a different expression of the same tragedy. During China's Cultural Revolution, children were taught that loyalty to the Communist Party was more important than loyalty to their parents, grandparents, teachers, or even truth itself. Students who had once stood respectfully when their teacher entered the classroom were encouraged to publicly accuse, humiliate, and sometimes brutally beat the very people who had devoted their lives to educating them. Neighbors informed on neighbors. Families were torn apart by suspicion and fear. The moral code that had governed society for centuries was swept away almost overnight and replaced by a new one, imposed not by conscience but by political power.

Again, the tragedy did not begin with violence.

It began when authority over morality changed hands.

The same pattern appeared in divided Germany after the Second World War. Families awoke to discover that a wall had risen through the heart of Berlin, separating husbands from wives, grandparents from grandchildren, lifelong friends from lifelong friends. The Berlin Wall was not built to keep enemies out. It was built to keep citizens from escaping. Hundreds lost their lives attempting to cross it because they believed that freedom was worth more than safety under a system that dictated every aspect of life. The concrete wall became a monument to a painful reality: when governments claim the authority to redefine truth and morality, they often discover that force is required to preserve the illusion.

That lesson remains visible even today.

Viewed from space at night, the Korean peninsula presents one of the most striking images on Earth. South Korea shines with the lights of vibrant cities stretching from coast to coast. North Korea, by contrast, is almost entirely dark. The two nations share the same peninsula, much of the same history, and generations of common ancestry. Yet they are separated by radically different ideas about authority, freedom, and truth. The darkness visible from orbit is more than a lack of electricity; it is a reminder that ideas eventually shape civilizations.

These stories are separated by continents, cultures, and decades, yet they all point to the same underlying truth. Totalitarian societies do not begin with concentration camps, labor camps, secret police, or prison walls. Those come later. They begin much earlier, when someone claims the authority to redefine morality itself—to declare that what was once good is now evil, what was once evil is now good, and that truth is no longer something to be discovered but something to be created.

If God is the Creator, then He is the ultimate authority, and truth, justice, and morality are discoveries. We do not invent them any more than we invent gravity or the laws of mathematics. But if humanity alone is the authority, then every generation—and eventually every individual—is left to construct its own version of truth. History shows that when that happens, confusion is never far behind.

The question before us is not whether morality will

govern our lives. It already does.

The question is who has the authority to define it.

The Conflict Over Authority

If God created humanity, then our nature, purpose, and moral boundaries are not inventions of culture or personal preference. They are realities that already exist. **We do not create them; we discover them.**

This is where the central conflict emerges.

Every generation eventually arrives at the same crossroads. Either truth is something we discover because it originates with God, or it is something we construct for ourselves through human reasoning, culture, or consensus.

The difference is profound.

If reality is God-defined, then truth exists whether we acknowledge it or not. If reality is human-defined, then truth becomes negotiable, changing with culture, circumstance, and opinion.

This conflict is not confined to philosophy classrooms or academic debates. It appears whenever societies struggle over questions such as:

- What is right and wrong?
- What gives human life value?
- Who determines identity?
- What is the purpose of human existence?

Behind each of these issues lies a more fundamental

one:

Who has the authority to define reality?

Scripture consistently points to God as the source of truth because He is the source of creation itself. We did not bring ourselves into existence. We are dependent beings—subordinate to the One who created us. Because God stands above creation, He alone sees reality completely and defines it perfectly.

When human beings embrace this truth, they gain a stable foundation for understanding life. When they reject it and attempt to place themselves in God's position, confusion inevitably follows. The Apostle Paul described the result this way:

> *"For although they knew God, they did not glorify Him as God or give thanks, but they became futile in their thoughts, and their senseless hearts were darkened." (Romans 1:21)*

History repeatedly demonstrates the truth of Paul's observation. Whenever humanity attempts to explain reality, morality, and meaning while excluding its Creator, confusion follows close behind. Some of the ideas that emerge can become remarkably detached from reality itself.

The Apple

Science seeks to understand the natural world through observation and analysis. Theology seeks to understand the spiritual realities and moral truths revealed by God. Each discipline has value on its own, but only together do they provide a complete picture of reality.

Imagine encountering an apple on the ground for the very first time, having no prior knowledge of what it is. You pick it up and take it home. Out of curiosity, you dissect it, examine its seeds, analyze its cells, and carefully record every detail.

Your investigation reveals much about the apple itself, yet your knowledge remains incomplete. Without knowing the tree it grew from, the soil that nourished it, or the climate that sustained it, you cannot fully explain its existence.

Studying nature apart from its Creator is much the same. We may accumulate impressive detail about the "apple"—the mechanisms of the natural world—but without recognizing its Source, we miss its greater meaning and purpose.

Human Reasoning has its Limits

A world solely governed by science and empirical observation without any moral or ethical standards could lead to some dark consequences, and potentially a complete disregard for human rights. Romans 1:21 gives a warning in this regard, when people excluded God, their "senseless hearts were darkened".

The Apostle Paul cautioned against using human reasoning to establish moral or theological values. In his letters to the Corinthians and Galatians, he wrote:

> *"We use God's mighty weapons, not worldly weapons, to knock down the strongholds of human reasoning and destroy false arguments." (2 Corinthians 10:4 NLT)*

> *"Dear brothers and sisters, I want you to understand that the gospel message that I preach is not based on mere human reasoning." (Galatians 1:11 NLT)*

Paul's own life defied human reasoning. He had been one of the greatest persecutors of Christians, tracking them down and terrorizing them. Acts 7:54-60 records his involvement in the stoning death of the Christian martyr Stephen.

His transformation from one who terrorized Christians to becoming a champion of Christians was sudden and complete when he encountered the resurrected Christ. It is by his own testimony that we know Christ transformed him in a single moment. That transformation through his encounter with Christ defies human reasoning. It also defies empirical and rational theory.

Isaac Newton and Enlightenment

When Isaac Newton died in 1727, England buried him among its greatest heroes in Westminster Abbey. To most people he was the scientist who explained gravity and changed the course of physics. Few realized that he devoted even more time studying Scripture than studying science.[6]

Newton never saw science and faith as competing explanations. To him they were partners. One revealed how creation worked; the other revealed why it existed.

Perhaps we should listen to what Newton wrote in "The Principia" regarding "The Rules of Reasoning in Philosophy":

> *"Therefore, to the same **natural effects** we must, as far as possible, **assign the same causes**." (emphasis added)*
>
> *"As to respiration in a man and in a beast; the descent of stones in Europe and in America; the light of our culinary fire and of the sun; the reflection of light in the earth, and in the planets."*[7]

Look carefully at the phrase written by Newton: "natural *effects*—assign the same *causes*". He is talking about the principle of "cause and effect", but is using it to explain that it is a fundamental concept in philosophy, science, and everyday *reasoning*.

How can we assign a cause if we fail to recognize the source of the cause as the Creator? Just as studying an apple without considering its tree gives an incomplete picture, studying creation without considering its Creator gives an

---

[6] Aron Heller, Israeli library uploads Newton's theological texts. (https://phys.org/news/2012-02-israeli-library-uploads-newton-theological.html) 2/15/2012.

[7] Newton, Isaac. THE MATHEMATICAL PRINCIPLES OF NATURAL PHILOSOPHY. Prometheus Books, New York. (1995). page 320.

incomplete understanding of reality.

The Rise of Enlightenment

Not long after Newton's death, the Age of Enlightenment introduced a dramatic shift in thinking. Philosophers such as Immanuel Kant began to argue that human reason—not divine revelation—should be the ultimate moral compass.[8]

Kant distrusted the senses, warning that they could easily mislead us.[9] He pointed to the ancient belief that the sun revolved around the earth as evidence that what we see is not always what is true. From there, he extended his skepticism to Scripture itself, suggesting that our own reasoning was more reliable than God's revealed Word.

At first glance, this approach seemed to elevate human dignity and intellectual freedom. But once human reason was made the final authority, truth itself became seen as unstable. If every individual can determine truth on their own terms, then truth is no longer fixed—it becomes fluid, shifting with culture, opinion, and circumstance.

History shows the consequences of this shift. The French Revolution, born from Enlightenment ideals, sought to cast off the authority of God and enthrone reason as supreme. Churches were desecrated, a "Goddess of Reason" was paraded through the streets, and centuries-old moral foundations were replaced with human invention. The result was not freedom but chaos—bloodshed, tyranny, and

---

[8] Kant, Immanuel. *An Answer to the Question: What is Enlightenment?* (1784). https://donelan.faculty.writing.ucsb.edu/enlight.html

[9] Kant, Immanuel. *Kant's Lectures on Anthropology*. Cambridge University Press. (Nov. 2014). Chapter 3.

moral collapse.[10] [11]

This is the essence of moral relativism. It replaces enduring standards with personal preference, leaving society without a solid foundation for justice or morality. What began as an appeal to human reason ended as a rejection of objective truth, with consequences still visible in the confusion and fragmentation of modern culture.[12]

Kant wrote of the Bible, “If I have a book to serve as my understanding… I need not think”.[13] To him, reason alone was enough. But history tells a different story: the Bible’s moral standards have guided societies toward stability, justice, and compassion for millennia.

When we replace God’s timeless truth with shifting human reasoning, we erode the moral foundation necessary for a healthy society. Moral relativism leads to fragmentation and confusion, while biblical principles offer a consistent framework for justice and unity.

Reason has great value, but it is not sufficient for determining morality. It must be anchored to something greater—something proven, enduring, and unchanging.

---

[10] Collins, Michael (1999). The Story of Christianity. Mathew A Price. Dorling Kindersley. pp. 176–177. ISBN 978-0-7513-0467-1.

[11] Kennedy, Emmet (1989). A Cultural History of the French Revolution. Yale University Press. p. 343. ISBN 9780300044263.

[12] Gowans, Chris, "Moral Relativism", The Stanford Encyclopedia of Philosophy (Spring 2021 Edition), Edward N. Zalta (ed.), URL = <https://plato.stanford.edu/archives/spr2021/entries/moral-relativism/>.

[13] Immanuel Kant. An Answer to the Question: What is Enlightenment? September 30, 1784.

Whose morality will it be?

History shows that civilizations rise or fall according to how they answer that question.

The Ukrainian farmer never intended to become part of history. The Berlin family never imagined a wall would divide their lives. The Chinese teacher never expected his own students to become his accusers.

Each simply lived in a society that answered one question differently.

Who has the authority to define morality?

Every generation must answer that question for itself.

So must every one of us.

Chapter 3: Summary

Every society answers the same question, whether it realizes it or not:

Who has the authority to define morality?

History shows that the answer shapes civilizations. When governments, cultures, or individuals assume the authority to redefine truth, morality, and human nature, confusion and suffering eventually follow. The tragedies of Ukraine, China, divided Germany, and North Korea remind us that ideas are never merely ideas. They shape families, nations, and generations.

If God is the Creator, then He is the ultimate authority,

and truth is not something we invent but something we discover. Just as an apple cannot be fully understood apart from the tree that produced it, creation cannot be fully understood apart from its Creator. Science helps us understand how the universe works, but Scripture reveals why it exists and what it means.

Human reason is one of God's greatest gifts, but it was never intended to replace the One who gave it. When reason is separated from its Source, truth becomes negotiable, morality becomes unstable, and every generation is left to construct reality for itself. When reason is anchored in God, it becomes a powerful tool for discovering the order, purpose, and meaning woven into creation.

The question before every generation—and every individual—is therefore the same:

Will we attempt to define truth, or will we discover the truth God has already established?

The answer shapes not only the world we build, but the people we become.

4 — Who Am I?

"So God created mankind in his own image, in the image of God he created them; male and female he created them."

Genesis 1:27

Bookstores are filled with books promising a better life. We read about leadership, productivity, influence, success, relationships, purpose, and personal growth. The desire to improve ourselves is nearly universal.

Yet beneath every effort at self-improvement lies a deeper question that is rarely asked:

Who exactly is the person being improved?

Before we can know where we are going, we must understand who we are. Before we can discover our purpose, we must understand our identity. Before we can improve ourselves, we must answer one of life's most fundamental questions:

Who am I?

Most people answer that question through achievements, relationships, possessions, careers, or personal beliefs. Scripture begins somewhere entirely different. It begins with God.

At the beginning of this journey together, we marveled at the truth that we are created in the image of God. Genesis 1:27 declares it plainly: "So God created mankind in his own image, in the image of God he created them; male and female he created them."

This alone is breathtaking. But Scripture reveals even deeper wonder and greater implications for our lives—especially as we consider our role in the Kingdom of God.

Not only are we made in His image, but we are crowned with majesty and glory. Psalm 8:5 tells us that God has made us "a little lower than the angels and crowned [us] with glory and honor."

This honor will eventually carry real authority for those in Christ: we will one day judge angels (1 Corinthians 6:3).

Yet even this remarkable privilege points to something even more astonishing about the way God has designed us. Angels, as magnificent as they are, are created servants. They do not create other angels. They cannot bring forth new life that bears the image of God.

Yet this is exactly what you and I can do. God has given humanity—unlike the angels—the remarkable ability to bring forth new life. Every child conceived, whether in the beauty of covenant marriage or in the brokenness of human failure, is still formed by God's sovereign hand.

He alone knits each one together in the womb (Psalm 139:13) and grants them a living spirit, an innate awareness of their Creator (Romans 1:20), and the potential to be filled with the Holy Spirit.

Every baby born is not merely a physical being, but a spiritual being with eternal destiny. In this sacred act, we reflect the creative heart of our Father in a way that even the angels cannot.

This is part of the profound purpose for which you were made. You are not an accident or a mere bystander in God's story. Though our sin nature has separated us from our Creator, in Christ we are welcomed home as sons and daughters of the King—redeemed and designed to reflect His glory, to create life that can know and love Him, and to one day reign with Him in His eternal Kingdom. What an honor! What a calling!

The next question is: what God do you believe in?

What God Do You Believe In?

> *"We proclaim to you what we have seen and heard, so that you also may have fellowship with us. And our fellowship is with the Father and with his Son, Jesus Christ."*
>
> *1 John 1:3*

It is entirely possible to say, "I believe in God," and yet

be speaking of something very different from the God of Scripture. For some, God is a force—something like energy woven into nature. For others, He is an abstract idea, the essence of humanity or the highest expression of what we value. Some picture Him as a distant Creator who set the universe in motion and then stepped back, never to engage again. Others, perhaps without realizing it, reshape God into a reflection of their own thoughts and ideals.

In each of these, God is acknowledged, but He is not truly known. He remains *impersonal*—something to consider, not Someone to encounter. And because of that, this kind of belief rarely changes anything. It may shape opinions, but it does not reshape a life.

A *personal* God is something altogether different—and this is exactly how the Bible presents Him. God is not an abstract idea or distant force. He is a personal being. He thinks. He possesses intellect. He chooses and acts according to His will. He relates, communicates, and engages with His creation. He moves within history, not outside of it.

This is not personality in the limited, human sense. It is something far greater—true personhood. It means that God is not merely to be studied or defined. He is a God who can be known.

This is where the distinction between an impersonal God and a personal God begins to matter in a very real way. If God is impersonal, then relationship is an illusion. There is no one to know, no one to respond to, and no one to whom we are accountable. Meaning becomes fragile, resting on human opinion rather than anything fixed or true. In the end, we are reduced to nothing more than physical existence—blood, bone, and tissue—living for a moment and then gone. Even prayer, in that framework, loses its meaning. It becomes words spoken into silence.

But if God is personal, everything shifts. You are no longer left to wonder in the abstract—you can know Him. Truth is no longer something we invent; it is grounded in His character. And that character is not hidden. It has been revealed. Your life is no longer without direction; it is tied to His will. He is sovereign, and we are accountable to Him.

In other words, once you move from the idea of God to the reality of a personal God, everything changes.

A Personal God

Why does it matter whether God is personal?

At first glance, the question may seem abstract or philosophical, but it reaches into nearly every part of life. The way we understand God ultimately shapes the way we understand ourselves. It influences how we think about truth, love, purpose, morality, and even our own worth.

Francis Schaeffer spent much of his life helping people think carefully about these questions. One of his most important observations was surprisingly simple: every worldview begins somewhere. Every person, whether religious or not, eventually arrives at a set of beliefs about what is ultimately real. The question is whether the foundation of reality is personal or impersonal.

Many modern explanations of the universe begin with

an impersonal foundation. Matter, energy, natural laws, and physical processes are viewed as the ultimate reality from which everything else has emerged. In that view, human beings are the result of a long chain of natural events. Personality, reason, morality, love, and purpose appear later as products of that process.

Yet when we step back and observe human experience, something interesting emerges. The things that matter most to us are not impersonal things. We care deeply about love, truth, justice, beauty, meaning, and relationships. We recognize kindness as better than cruelty. We admire courage, honesty, sacrifice, and compassion. We instinctively believe that human life possesses value and dignity.

Schaeffer encouraged people to follow an idea to its logical conclusion. If reality is ultimately impersonal, where do these deeply personal realities come from? How does purpose arise from a universe that has no purpose? How does objective meaning emerge from a process that has no intention? Why should love be regarded as something noble rather than merely useful?

These questions do not prove God exists, but they do point us toward something important. The realities we treasure most—love, reason, morality, meaning, and human dignity—are personal in nature. They fit naturally within a universe created by a personal God.

Scripture begins with exactly that foundation.

Before there was a universe, there was God. Before there was matter, energy, space, or time, there was One who knew, loved, chose, communicated, and created. Personality did not emerge from creation; personality existed before creation because it existed in the Creator.

This helps explain why human beings are unlike anything else in the physical world. We are not merely biological organisms. We are image-bearers. Our capacity to reason, to create, to communicate, to love, and to seek meaning reflects something of the One who made us.

It also explains why Scripture places such value on every human life. Human worth is not determined by intelligence, appearance, wealth, social status, ability, or achievement. It is not something earned through performance. It is something bestowed by God. Every person possesses inherent dignity because every person bears the image of the Creator.

Love itself becomes easier to understand within this framework. The Bible does not present love as something humanity invented. It presents love as something we reflect. As Scripture says, "We love because He first loved us" (1 John 4:19). Love is not merely a biological mechanism or a survival strategy. It is rooted in the character of a personal God whose nature is love.

This understanding changes the way we answer the question, "Who am I?"

If ultimate reality is impersonal, identity ultimately becomes something we must create for ourselves. We spend our lives searching for meaning, value, and purpose, hoping to discover something solid on which to stand.

But if a personal Creator exists, identity is not something we invent. It is something we discover. Our worth is not self-defined. Our purpose is not self-assigned. The One who created us has already spoken to these questions.

That is why the difference between a personal God and an impersonal universe is far more than an intellectual debate. It affects how we understand ourselves, how we value others, and how we make sense of the world around us.

And if God truly is personal, the next question naturally follows:

Can He be known?

How We Know a Personal God

We know God because He has made Himself known. We are not left to search in the dark or piece Him together through speculation. God has spoken first. He has revealed Himself through His creation—in what has been made. He has revealed Himself in Scripture—in what He has said. And He has revealed Himself most clearly in Jesus Christ—in who He is.

In Christ, we begin to see God's nature in a way we can grasp. We see His character, His compassion, His authority, and His purpose. We also begin to understand something about ourselves—what it means to be made in His image, and what God intended from the beginning. When He created Adam, His design was not distance, but fellowship. Not isolation, but relationship. We were created to walk with Him and to live in faithful stewardship of what He has made.

So knowing God is not a matter of guessing or constructing ideas. It is a response to what He has already revealed.

Knowing God is also not merely an intellectual exercise. A person can study theology, memorize Scripture, and still remain distant. Information alone does not bring relationship. To truly know a personal God means engaging Him as a living Person, not as a concept to be understood.

As that relationship grows, what is true about God begins to take shape in you—in your faith, in your trust, and in the way you see your life. You begin to recognize His sovereignty not in theory, but in the ordinary moments—in each day, each decision, even each breath. Knowing God becomes an ongoing interaction, not something reserved for study or for moments of desperation.

It is the difference between knowing facts about someone and actually knowing them. You may know when a person was born. You may read their story. But that kind of knowledge is very different from the relationship between a parent and a child—walking together, caring, interacting, sharing life. That kind of knowing goes far beyond information. It is personal, continuous, and real.

The experience of knowing God is real. It is not something confined to a Sunday morning or reduced to doctrine on a page. It is truth—something that can be lived and experienced. Not in a mystical or distant way, but in the reality of everyday life.

God's presence is not abstract. It can be known in the ordinary rhythms of life. Prayer becomes more than a ritual;

it becomes real communication. As we live under His sovereignty, obedience begins to shape us. Change takes place—not just inwardly, but in ways that can be seen.

Through faith in Christ, the Holy Spirit works within us, producing a transformation that would not be possible on our own. Character is formed. Life is redirected. What emerges is something real and lasting—the fruit of a relationship lived moment by moment with God.

Our Living Connection to God

Jesus promised that the Holy Spirit would dwell within us, not just as a concept but as a living presence who teaches, reminds, and reveals truth (John 14:26; John 16:13).

The Spirit is not distant. He intercedes when we struggle to pray (Romans 8:26), confirms our identity as God's children (Romans 8:16), and gives us direct access to the Father (Ephesians 2:18). Through Him, we experience a relationship with God that is personal, intimate, and continual.

As we walk by the Spirit, we are led away from the chaos of self-centered living into a life marked by love, peace, and purpose (Galatians 5:16, 22–23). He is the One who makes our relationship with God real—not theoretical—and empowers us to live as image-bearers who reflect God's character in a broken world.

The Holy Spirit is not just a doctrine; He is the vital link between belief and transformation. Through Him, we are reminded that our identity is not only defined by God—it is sustained by His presence within us.

The New Creation: Who Am I In Christ?

This brings us to the most personal and beautiful part of our identity. Everything we've explored so far—being made in God's image, crowned with honor, and designed for relationship with Him—finds its fullest expression here.

The apostle Paul captured this transforming reality in one of the most hopeful verses in all of Scripture:

> *"Therefore, if anyone is in Christ, he is a new creature; the old things passed away; behold, new things have come." (2 Corinthians 5:17 NASB)*

Notice those two powerful words: **in Christ**. This is not about working harder to become a better version of yourself. It's not an emotional high or an instant personality makeover. It is a profound, relational, and positional change. When you move from self-rule to trusting the King, your standing before God is altered—instantly and forever.

So what exactly changes?

Paul is wonderfully clear. The "old things" that pass away are not your personality, your memories, or even your struggles. What passes away is your old position—your identity in Adam, your separation from God, and your slavery to sin. You are no longer defined by condemnation. A real transfer of authority has taken place. You are no longer enslaved. You are free.

This is the amazing difference: before Christ, a person has only one nature—the fallen one we all inherit. But when you are *in Christ*, something astonishing happens. You now have two natures living side by side. The old nature still whispers familiar lies and pulls at old habits. But it no longer owns you. You have been liberated. You now have a genuine choice—and the Holy Spirit living within you—to say yes to the King.

Think of John Newton, the former slave trader who became a pastor and wrote "Amazing Grace." The man didn't disappear. His personality, gifts, and even some of his struggles remained. But everything was brought under new authority. The same is true for you.

Many believers have stumbled here, expecting the new creation to erase every struggle the moment they believe. When the old temptations return—and they do—they wonder if anything really happened. The old nature still fights for the throne it once ruled. The new nature bows before the rightful King. That inner struggle you sometimes feel? It's not a sign that nothing has changed. It's beautiful evidence that something has changed. You are alive in a way you never were before.

You are no longer defined by Adam's condemnation or spiritual death. A transfer of authority has occurred. You are no longer enslaved. You are now free.

In Christ, you now have capacities you never had on your own. Your spirit has been made alive. The Holy Spirit Himself has taken up residence in you. You have access to the mind of Christ. You can grow in love, wisdom, and obedience in ways that once seemed impossible.

Of course, these are capacities, not automatic results. The old patterns don't vanish overnight. That's why Paul encourages us to "be transformed by the renewing of your mind" (Romans 12:2). Growth happens day by day as you choose the King you now know.

When the old temptations return and you feel the pull, you no longer have to question whether you are truly saved. You simply need to remember—you are no longer defined by that old nature. You belong to Christ. The same dignity celebrated in Psalm 8 is still yours—now empowered by the Spirit of the King.

You were made a little lower than the angels and crowned with glory and majesty so you could rule under God's authority. That purpose was always there. Sin interrupted it, but it did not cancel it. In Christ, it becomes possible again.

The new creation is not about becoming someone else. It is about becoming the person God always intended you to be—fully alive, deeply loved, fully accountable, and finally free to live for the Kingdom you were created to serve.

This new identity does not rest on your performance. It rests securely on the reliable Word of the God who created you and has now re-created you in Christ.

And that leads us naturally to the next honest question every seeker must face: Can we really trust what God has said?

You Are Not Self-Created

Every human being eventually asks the question: Who am I?

The world offers many answers. Scripture gives one.

You are created in the image of God.

You are not a biochemical accident.
You are not a cosmic coincidence.
You are not the byproduct of blind forces.

Your worth is not negotiated.
It is given.
Your dignity is not earned.
It is inherent.
Your identity is not self-constructed.
It is God-established.

When identity is anchored in the Creator,
it becomes stable.
You know who you are.
And you know whose you are.

The One who said, "Let there be light,"
also said, "Let us make mankind in Our image."

You are not self-created.
You are God-created.
And that changes everything.

"For God so loved the world that he gave his one and only Son, that whoever believes in him shall not perish but have eternal life." John 3:16

Chapter 4: Summary

This chapter begins with one of life's most important questions: **Who am I?**

The world often answers that question through achievement, relationships, possessions, status, or personal beliefs. Scripture begins somewhere very different. It begins with God.

The Bible teaches that every human being is created in the image of God. Because of that, our worth, dignity, and purpose are not earned or self-created. They are gifts bestowed by our Creator. We are not accidents, byproducts of chance, or forgotten participants in a meaningless universe. We were intentionally created by God and designed for relationship with Him.

This chapter also explores an important distinction: the difference between a personal God and an impersonal view of reality. If ultimate reality is impersonal, meaning, love, morality, and human dignity become difficult to explain. But if the foundation of reality is a personal Creator, then the deepest realities of human experience make sense. Love reflects His nature. Purpose reflects His design. Human value reflects His image.

Because God is personal, He is not merely a concept to be studied. He can be known. God has revealed Himself through creation, through Scripture, and most clearly through Jesus Christ. Through faith in Christ and the indwelling presence of the Holy Spirit, we can experience a genuine relationship with the One who created us.

For those who trust Christ, identity reaches its fullest expression in the new creation. We are no longer defined by separation from God or by the authority of sin. We are made new. Though the struggle between the old and new natures remains, that struggle is evidence that something real has changed. We belong to Christ and are being transformed into the people God intended us to be.

In the end, the answer to **Who am I?** is not found by looking inward or constructing an identity for ourselves.

You are created in the image of God.

You are known by a personal Creator.

And in Christ, you are made new.

5 — The Reliability of God's Word

> *"All Scripture is God-breathed and is useful for teaching, rebuking, correcting and training in righteousness, so that the servant of God may be thoroughly equipped for every good work."*
>
> *2 Timothy 3:16*

If you are created in the image of God...

If you are known and loved by a personal Creator...

If you are made new in Christ...

Then everything hinges on one foundational question: Has God truly spoken? And can we trust what He has said?

Chapter 4 reminded us who we are. But identity alone is not enough. For that identity to be secure, its source must be secure. If the God who calls us His image-bearers is silent, or if His words cannot be trusted, then even the most beautiful truths about who we are eventually become uncertain. Our dignity, our purpose, our hope of transformation—all of it rests on whether God has spoken clearly and reliably.

This is why the reliability of Scripture is not a side issue for theologians. It is intensely personal. It touches the very ground we stand on when we say, "I am known by God." Because if Scripture is the foundation of the Christian worldview, then everything that follows: our understanding of life, ethics, suffering, forgiveness, eternity, and meaning —rises or falls on whether God's Word is true.

Science, History, and the Reliability of Scripture

Many people assume there is a conflict between science and theology. The Bible is often dismissed as mythology, while science is viewed as the realm of measurable facts. But this contrast is misleading.

Science is a method for discovering truth about the physical world through observation, testing, and verification. Historical scholarship applies similar principles to documents: examining manuscripts, comparing sources, evaluating dating, and testing consistency. In both fields, claims are evaluated by evidence.

When those same standards are applied to the New Testament, something unexpected happens. Instead of collapsing under scrutiny, the text strengthens. The manuscript evidence is vast. The transmission is transparent. Variations are documented and analyzed. Core doctrines remain intact across thousands of copies.

The idea that Scripture survives only because it was blindly preserved by religious tradition does not withstand historical examination. The Bible is not shielded from investigation. It has been studied, questioned, compared, and tested more than any other ancient document in history.

Archaeology further confirms this reliability. For example, the Pool of Bethesda, described in John 5:2 as a place with five porticoes where Jesus healed a paralyzed man, was long doubted by critics who claimed no such site existed in Jerusalem. Excavations in the 19th and 20th centuries uncovered the exact location north of the Temple Mount — two large pools divided by a wall, with porticoes (covered colonnades) on four sides and one in the middle, precisely matching the biblical description. This discovery shows that the Gospel writer had detailed, accurate knowledge of first-century Jerusalem.

The perceived conflict, then, is not between science and Scripture. It is between assumption and evidence. When we examine the historical facts with the same intellectual honesty we apply to scientific claims, the label "mythology" becomes increasingly difficult to sustain.

The Christian Worldview

The Christian worldview is centered on the teachings of Jesus Christ, which we learn from the New Testament. Our confidence in His teachings rests on the authenticity and accuracy of the New Testament manuscripts and the reliability of modern translations.

For nearly 1,400 years after the New Testament was completed, every copy had to be written by hand. These *manuscripts*—roughly 400 pages long—were rare, time-consuming to produce, and carefully guarded. Then came the printing press in 1440, followed by our modern Information Age, where entire libraries can be duplicated and shared in seconds.

Today, organizations like the Center for the Study of New Testament Manuscripts (CSNTM), founded by Dr. Daniel Wallace, are using digital technology to locate, photograph, and analyze every known handwritten copy. Their work provides compelling evidence that modern translations reflect the original documents with remarkable accuracy.

For example, the King James Version (KJV), published in 1611, was based on only eight Greek manuscripts, none earlier than the 11th century.[14] In contrast, today's translations draw from more than 5,600 Greek manuscripts—some dating to the second century—along with over 10,000 Latin manuscripts. This represents roughly 687 times more source material than was available in 1611, allowing scholars to cross-check and refine the text with far greater precision, thus improving rather than diminishing the accuracy of modern translations.[15]

King James Bible (1611 AD):

- 8 Greek Manuscripts
- Earliest Manuscript, ~ 1100 AD

---

[14] KJVBibles. New Testament Manuscripts And The KJV. https://www.kjvbibles.com/new-testament-manuscripts-and-the-kjv

[15] Dr. Daniel Wallace lecture at the Text and Canon Institute. Is What We Have Now What They Wrote Then? (March 21, 2020). https://www.youtube.com/watch?v=FHP9aNDXDTw

Current Translations:

- 5,600+ Greek Manuscripts
- 10,000+ Latin Manuscripts
- Earliest Manuscript, before 200 AD

In addition, tens of thousands of quotations from early church fathers are so extensive that the entire New Testament could be reconstructed many times over from them alone.

When compared to other ancient writings, the difference is striking. All surviving copies of Aristotle, Plato, and Herodotus combined would stack about four feet high. The Greek New Testament manuscripts alone would reach over 6,600 feet (more than 1.25 miles).[16]

While the authenticity of classical Greek philosophers is rarely questioned, the New Testament—despite having exponentially more evidence—still faces skepticism. Yet it records not abstract ideas, but the life, death, and resurrection of Jesus Christ, the most consequential person in human history.

Is the New Testament Accurate?

An important question arises: *Is what we have today truly what was originally written?*

Consider the Gettysburg Address, delivered by President

---

[16] Dr. Daniel B. Wallace. How Tall Would a Stack of New Testament Manuscripts Be? (Jan. 1, 2023). https://danielbwallace.com/2023/01/01/how-tall-would-a-stack-of-new-testament-manuscripts-be/

Abraham Lincoln. The original version no longer exists. Instead, we have five copies made by Lincoln's associates. Even the version displayed in the Lincoln Room of the White House is not the original—it's a handwritten copy Lincoln created at the request of Colonel Alexander Bliss.[17] Each of the five versions differs slightly in wording, yet all are regarded as faithful reflections of the original speech. Similarly, we don't need the original Greek New Testament to preserve and share the teachings of Christ. The copies we have are exceptionally reliable.

The New Testament is preserved in a far stronger position.

When scholars compare thousands of Greek manuscripts, they do find textual variants. That is expected whenever documents are copied by hand. However, the overwhelming majority of these differences involve spelling, word order, or minor grammatical changes. In Greek, word order is flexible, so rearranging words often leaves the meaning unchanged. As Dr. Daniel Wallace notes, there are over 100 ways to say "John loves Mary" in Greek, all expressing the same idea.

When textual scholars speak of "meaningful" variants, they do not mean every difference in wording. They refer specifically to variations that could potentially affect the meaning of a passage and that have some plausible manuscript support. By that definition, less than 0.1% of the New Testament text contains any meaningful and viable

---

[17] American Battlefield Trust. Versions of the Gettysburg Address. (November 16, 2023). https://www.battlefields.org/learn/articles/versions-gettysburg-address

variation—and even within that small fraction, no core doctrine of the Christian faith is placed in doubt.

For example, in Mark 9:29:

> *"And He said to them, 'This kind cannot come out by anything but prayer [and fasting].'"*

The phrase "and fasting" appears in some later manuscripts but is absent in the earliest and most reliable copies. Because we possess thousands of manuscripts for comparison, such additions are easily detected and noted in modern translations. The transparency of this process is not a weakness—it is evidence of careful scholarship.

For this reason, we can speak with approximately 99.9% confidence in the textual stability of the New Testament and with full confidence that its theological message has been faithfully preserved. Reliable modern translations such as the NASB, NET, NIV, and others are based on a manuscript tradition that has been examined more thoroughly than any other ancient work.

The New Testament's accuracy is not a fragile assumption. It is the result of extensive manuscript evidence, rigorous comparison, and centuries of careful scholarship—allowing us to engage the Word of God with confidence that what we are reading reflects what was originally written.

There's No Other Book Like the Bible

While its reliability is remarkable, the Bible is also utterly unique among ancient texts.

Its sheer age sets it apart. Most books barely survive from one generation to the next before fading into obscurity. By contrast, the earliest chapters of the Bible were written during the era when the great pyramids of Egypt were being constructed. The oldest biblical texts are approximately 3,500 years old, and the entirety of Scripture was written over a span of about 1,500 years.

Imagine trying to publish a single, coherent book that would take more than 1,500 years to complete. No single author, editor, or publishing house could possibly see it through. You would need a continuous chain of committed people across dozens of generations, surviving wars, empires, plagues, and cultural upheavals, all while preserving the same core message with remarkable consistency. History shows how rare such long-term continuity is: most nations and governments struggle to last even 250 years without major collapse or transformation. Yet the biblical writings endured.

Physical monuments from the ancient world often crumble. The pyramids themselves, once gleaming wonders, have weathered thousands of years of wind, sand, and time. But the Bible has not only survived—it has thrived as a living document, actively read, copied, studied, and applied in every generation.

This combination of extreme antiquity, multi-generational authorship, and unbroken preservation through millennia of turmoil makes the Bible truly one of a kind. No other book in human history matches its longevity, resilience, and enduring relevance. It stands not merely as a historical artifact, but as a living testament to God's providential care, pointing every generation to the same unchanging God who inspired it.

What Motivated the Authors of the Bible?

The men who wrote the Bible were driven by something far greater than money, fame, or personal comfort. They received no payment and sought no worldly reward. Instead, they willingly endured rejection, persecution, and even death to proclaim God's truth.

Many paid the ultimate price. According to church tradition, Peter and Andrew were crucified, James was stoned, Matthew was martyred, Jude was killed with an axe, and prophets like Jeremiah and Habakkuk were also stoned. Even Jesus Himself was crucified for the message He proclaimed—a message His followers then recorded at great peril to themselves.

What gave them such courage? They were not writing second-hand rumors or clever philosophy. The apostles in particular were eyewitnesses of the resurrected Christ. They had seen Him alive after His crucifixion, touched His wounds, shared meals with Him, and received His commission. That firsthand encounter transformed them from fearful men into bold witnesses willing to die rather than deny what they had personally seen and heard (see 1 John 1:1-3). Their writings were not the product of ambition, but of conviction rooted in divine inspiration and undeniable experience.

This costly commitment explains why their words endured. In hostile cultures that often rejected God's truth, these authors wrote with a passion and authority that no human motive could sustain. Their sacrifice, under God's providence, preserved a message that continues to change lives today.

Unity and Continuity of Ideas

One of the Bible's most remarkable attributes is its profound unity and continuity of ideas, maintained across more than 1,500 years despite being written by approximately 40 different authors.

These writers came from radically diverse backgrounds: uneducated fishermen like Peter and John, a shepherd like Amos, a tax collector like Matthew, priests and rabbis, physicians like Luke, statesmen and kings like David and Solomon, and even a cupbearer to a pagan king like Nehemiah. They lived in different nations, spoke different languages, and wrote under vastly different circumstances—some in palaces, others in prisons or deserts. Their life experiences ranged from royal luxury to slavery and exile.

In any ordinary human project, such diversity would almost guarantee disagreement, contradiction, or fragmentation. Think how hard it is today to get even a small group of people from similar backgrounds to agree on important issues. Yet these 40 authors, spread across fifteen centuries, produced a single, harmonious message: one consistent story of creation, humanity's fall, God's redemptive plan, and the coming of the Messiah.

The odds of this kind of unity happening by chance are astronomical. This is no mere coincidence. It reflects the guiding hand of one divine Author—the Holy Spirit—superintending each human writer, ensuring that Scripture speaks with a single, unified voice.

From Genesis to Revelation: One Story

There is a powerful image that portrays the Bible's unity: a rainbow sweeping across the pages of Scripture, with 63,779 arcs connecting verses, ideas, people, and promises.[18] At first glance, it looks like artwork. But look closer, and you see something breathtaking: the story of God's Word linking together in one continuous message.

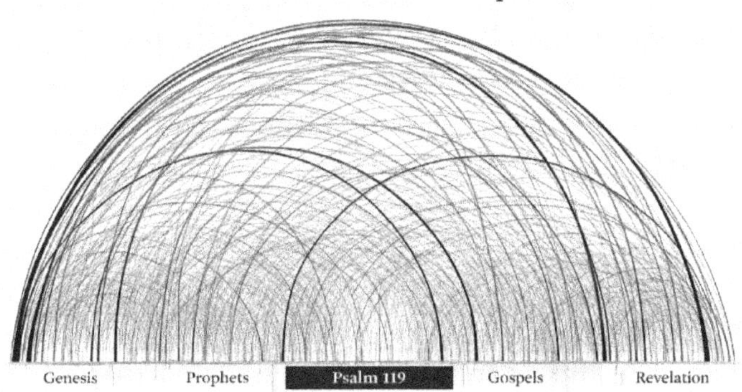

Credit: Bible Cross-References. Chris Harrison

The arcs stretch from the earliest pages of Genesis to the final words of Revelation, reminding us that the Bible is not a collection of scattered writings, but one unfolding story—God re-establishing His kingdom and choosing to work through mankind to accomplish it.

[18] Chris Harrison. Bible Cross-References. https://www.chrisharrison.net/index.php/Visualizations/BibleViz

At the center of this rainbow lies a long, light-gray bar representing Psalm 119, the Bible's longest chapter. Its 176 verses, divided into 22 sections for each letter of the Hebrew alphabet, symbolize completeness. The psalmist's use of the entire alphabet declares that God's Word is whole, comprehensive, and sufficient for every part of life.

The colors of the arcs show how far apart the connected passages are, and they remind us of something astonishing: an ancient prophecy in one book finds its fulfillment centuries later in another. For example, Isaiah's vision of the Suffering Servant—"He was pierced for our transgressions, He was crushed for our iniquities" (Isaiah 53:5)—finds its fulfillment in the Gospels' account of Jesus' crucifixion. This is only one of thousands of connections, all pointing us to Christ, the center of the story.

What might seem like 40 authors scattered over 1,545 years is revealed to be something much greater: one divine Author weaving a single, unified narrative. The rainbow of Scripture does not simply decorate the page—it reveals the faithfulness of God, the harmony of His Word, and the glory of His kingdom breaking into history through Jesus Christ.

Another image takes this truth even further by focusing on the Psalms and their relationship to the New Testament.[19] Instead of isolated songs and prayers, the Psalms are shown to be woven directly into the life and ministry of Jesus and echoed in the writings of the apostles.

---

[19] OpenBible. Bible Cross References Visualization. https://www.openbible.info/labs/cross-references/visualization?from=Ps&to=NT

Psalms Interwoven with the New Testament

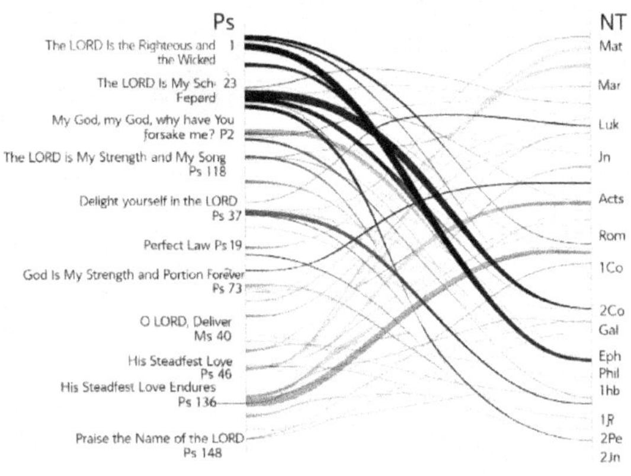

Credit: Bible Cross References Visualization. Open Bible.

Consider Psalm 22, which begins: *"My God, my God, why have You forsaken me?"* David first voiced these words in anguish. Centuries later, Jesus spoke them from the cross (Matthew 27:46), fulfilling them in a way David himself could never have imagined. What began as lament became prophecy, brought to completion in Christ's suffering and triumph.

When we see these connections drawn out visually, we begin to understand something extraordinary: Scripture speaks with one voice across more than 1,500 years of history, through 40 different authors from radically different backgrounds. Normally, such diversity would fracture into competing stories and conflicting perspectives. But the Bible holds together with one unified theme: the story of God's kingdom, humanity's redemption, and the reign of Christ.

Empires rose and fell during the time the Bible was

being written. Languages changed, cultures evolved, and worldviews shifted. Yet the message of Scripture never broke apart. Instead, it held together with a guiding unity that transcends human ability. Its consistency is not only unusual — it is miraculous.

This continuity is not just literary; it is theological. If the Bible were simply a human work, we would expect contradictions and competing ideas. Instead, it unfolds seamlessly: creation, fall, redemption through Christ, and the promised restoration of all things.

Together, these images — the rainbow of Scripture and the web connecting Psalms to the New Testament — reveal more than just data points. They testify to the divine authorship of the Bible. Forty human authors across fifteen centuries could not have orchestrated such harmony. Only one divine Author could weave this story: God Himself, revealing His plan through His Word and bringing it to fulfillment in His Son.

The Bible is not just connected; it is alive, speaking with a single voice, telling one story from Genesis to Revelation: the story of God's kingdom, restored through Christ, into which we are invited.

Why the Bible is Relevant to You

Self-help literature has gained immense popularity in recent decades, and many influential authors openly acknowledge that their wisdom is rooted in the truths of Scripture.

Dale Carnegie, author of *How to Win Friends and*

Influence People, sold more than 30 million copies of his book and credited much of his insight to what he called "the great spiritual truths that all churches teach."[1] His widely adopted principles—humility, empathy, restraint, encouragement—echo teachings found in Scripture.[20]

Stephen Covey's *The 7 Habits of Highly Effective People*, translated into dozens of languages and read by millions worldwide, was shaped by his daily meditation on Scripture. Covey viewed the Bible not as an abstract religious text, but as the foundation of his value system and leadership philosophy.[21]

The same pattern appears elsewhere. Rick Warren's *The Purpose Driven Life* and Dave Ramsey's financial principles are explicitly grounded in biblical teaching. Warren's work has sold tens of millions of copies, and Ramsey's approach to stewardship has reshaped how families think about debt, discipline, and responsibility.

Even in the world of management theory, Scripture's influence is evident. Peter Drucker—often called the father of modern management—acknowledged that his Christian faith shaped the principles he taught.[4] Concepts such as stewardship, responsibility, service-oriented leadership, and accountability are not modern inventions; they are deeply biblical ideas.[22]

---

[20] Carnegie, Dale. *How to Stop Worrying and Start Living*. Chapter 19. Simon & Schuster. (July 30, 2010).

[21] Covey, Stephen R. *The 7 Habits of Highly Effective People*. Simon & Schuster. (1989). Pages 292-293.

[22] "On Point" (radio show). Host Tom Ashbrook. *Drucker described himself as a "very conventional, traditional Christian," emphasizing a simple, obedient faith by saying, "My job is to say, 'Yes, sir.'" He found comfort in this faith and expressed gratitude daily with the phrase,*

The point is not that these leaders replaced Scripture. It is that they drew from it.

What millions embrace today as "best practices" in leadership, relationships, finance, and personal growth often reflects principles that have been preserved in the Bible for thousands of years.

The Bible is not merely a devotional text. It addresses how humans flourish, how authority should function, how responsibility should be carried, and how relationships should be ordered. Its influence is woven into modern thought more deeply than many realize.

But Scripture does more than improve productivity or strengthen leadership. It points beyond techniques and habits to the One who defines truth itself. It speaks not only to success, but to meaning. Not only to discipline, but to redemption.

In a rapidly shifting world, the Bible remains uniquely stable—offering not just strategies for living well, but a foundation for understanding reality, identity, and hope.

If God Has Spoken

Chapter 4 established who you are: an image-bearer, created by God.

This chapter answers the next necessary question: Has that God actually spoken—and can we trust what He

---

"Praise be to God for the beauty of his creation. Amen" (Drucker, then 95 years old - December 2004).

said?

The evidence is not thin. It is overwhelming.

Thousands of Greek manuscripts.
Thousands more in Latin.

Quotations from early church fathers sufficient to reconstruct the New Testament many times over.

Manuscripts dating within generations of the originals.
Minor variations.
No doctrine altered.
No theology lost.

The New Testament is not fragile. It is reinforced.

When compared to other ancient works—Aristotle, Plato and Herodotus—the manuscript support is not comparable. It is exponentially greater.

The Bible is not a collection of moral reflections. It is a historical claim.

It declares that Jesus lived.
That He was crucified.
That He rose from the dead.
That eyewitnesses recorded it.
And that those eyewitnesses were willing to suffer and die rather than deny what they had seen.

This is not mythology slowly formed in obscurity.
It is testimony preserved in abundance.

If Scripture were unreliable, Christianity collapses.

But if Scripture is reliable—as the evidence strongly supports—then its claims demand a response.

Because the Bible does not merely inform you—it confronts you.

It says you are created.
It says you are accountable.
It says you are loved.
It says you are redeemable.
It says history is moving toward a restored kingdom.

And it anchors those claims in a person—Jesus Christ.

You can dismiss the Bible.
But you cannot dismiss it honestly without examining it.

The manuscripts are there.
The continuity is there.
The preservation is there.
The historical claim is there.

If God has spoken—and the evidence says He has—then the most important question is no longer about textual variants.

It is about a personal relationship with Christ.

Because the reliability of God's Word is not merely a scholarly conclusion.

It is the foundation upon which your identity, your morality, your hope, and your eternity stand.

And if that foundation is secure—everything changes.

Chapter 5: Summary

This chapter asks a critical question: *Has God truly spoken—and can we trust what He has said?*

If identity is grounded in God, then it must also be grounded in something stable. Scripture claims to be that foundation, but its reliability must be examined, not assumed. When it is, the evidence is striking. The New Testament is supported by an extraordinary number of manuscripts, preserved with transparency, and tested through centuries of careful study. Instead of weakening under scrutiny, it proves remarkably stable.

This reliability is not only textual—it is historical. The Bible stands apart from other ancient writings in both the volume of evidence and the consistency of its message. It is not a fragile tradition passed down blindly, but a record examined, compared, and preserved with precision.

At the same time, the Bible is unique in its unity. Written over more than a thousand years by many authors from different backgrounds, it tells one consistent story—pointing to God's kingdom and fulfilled in Jesus Christ. That continuity is not easily explained by human effort alone.

The question, then, is not simply whether the Bible exists, but whether it can be trusted. And if it can be trusted, its message cannot be ignored. Scripture does not merely offer ideas—it makes claims about reality, about who you are, and about what God has done through Christ.

In the end, the issue becomes personal. If God has spoken, then His Word carries authority. And if His Word is reliable, then it forms the foundation for everything that follows—your identity, your understanding of truth, and your relationship with Him.

6 — When God Reveals Himself

"And behold, a severe earthquake had occurred, for an angel of the Lord descended from heaven and came and rolled away the stone, and sat upon it. And his appearance was like lightning, and his clothing as white as snow. The guards shook from fear of him and became like dead men."

Matthew 28:2–4

Chapter 5 established that Scripture is reliable. The testimony is preserved. The message is unified. But reliability is not the end of the matter. It is the beginning.

Because once we trust the record, we must ask a deeper question:

Why does God reveal Himself at all?

The burning bush was not merely light in a desert.
It was a call.

The radiant face of Moses was not spectacle.
It was authority confirmed.

The resurrection was not display.
It was victory declared.

In every case, when God steps into history, He does so with purpose. He reveals Himself in order to call, to rescue, to confirm, to warn, to redeem—us. Miracles are not curiosities. They are invitations.

And if that is true, then the question is no longer about whether miracles happened.

The question becomes whether God is still revealing Himself—and whether we are listening.

Moses and the Burning Bush

> *"So Moses said, "I must turn aside now and see this marvelous sight, why the bush is not burned up." When the LORD saw that he turned aside to look, God called to him from the midst of the bush and said, "Moses, Moses!" And he said, "Here I am.""*
>
> *Exodus 3:3-4*

Moses was out tending sheep near Mount Horeb when something stopped him in his tracks. An ordinary bush was on fire—flames dancing all over it—but the bush itself wasn't burning up. It wasn't turning to ash. It just kept shining.

Curious, Moses stepped closer. That's when he heard the voice of God calling his name from the middle of the flames.

The Lord declares the ground holy, reveals His plan to rescue Israel from slavery in Egypt, and commissions Moses—despite his protests of inadequacy—to lead His people. God promises to support Moses with His presence and confirming signs.

That moment changed everything.

From a simple, everyday perspective, fire normally consumes its fuel until only ashes remain. The heat excites atoms, which release photons—the little packets of light we see as flames. But this bush was different. It kept giving off bright light and heat without being consumed. Something was supplying steady energy to keep those photons streaming out—energy that wasn't coming from the bush itself being eaten away.

This is where the miracle meets the deeper truth of who God is. In Genesis 1:3, God didn't need fuel or any created thing. He simply said, "Let there be light," and there was light. He is the Creator of energy itself.

In the burning bush, God was personally present, supplying the energy that sustained the flames. The atoms in the bush released the visible photons, but the power behind them came from the One who spoke the universe into being. He didn't destroy the bush—He sustained it. He stepped into the natural order and showed His authority over it.

That's the heart of the moment. The burning bush was holy ground where the eternal God revealed Himself to a man. The same God who met Moses in that unconsumed flame is the One whose fingerprints are all over quantum energy, motion, relativity, and even black holes.

When He reveals Himself, He does it with purpose—to call us, to commission us, and to show us that He is both near and sovereign. The question for us is the same one Moses faced: Will we turn aside and listen when the Creator speaks through both His Word and His works?

The Radiant Face of Moses

> *"When Aaron and all the Israelites saw Moses, his face was radiant, and they were afraid to come near him.."*
>
> *Exodus 34:29-35*

After forty days and nights in God's presence on Mount Sinai, Moses descended carrying the tablets of the law. He didn't realize it, but his face was shining with a bright, radiant light—intense enough to terrify the people. They drew back until Moses called them near, delivered God's commands, and then veiled his face. He removed the veil only when he returned to speak with the Lord.

This wasn't ordinary sunlight. It was a visible afterglow of being in the glory of God Himself.

Living things naturally emit very faint biophotons, but they are invisible. Moses' face emitted strong, visible light—bright enough to inspire fear. The atoms in his skin released photons at levels far beyond normal biology, yet his face remained undamaged and healthy. Something was supplying a steady stream of energy that wasn't coming from his own body.

This echoes the burning bush. The same Creator who

spoke light into existence supplied divine energy that caused Moses' living skin to shine without harm. The atoms released the photons we could see, but the power came directly from God's presence.

The radiant face of Moses was confirmation. The light visibly announced, "This man has stood in the presence of the living God. Listen to the words he brings." It gave tangible proof of divine authority.

The same God who caused Moses' face to shine is the One whose fingerprints we will trace through quantum energy, motion, relativity, and black holes. When God reveals Himself—whether through a burning bush or a radiant face—He does it with purpose: to call us, to confirm His authority, and to draw us into deeper relationship with Him. The question for every one of us is the same one the Israelites faced: Will we draw near when we see the evidence of His presence?

The Birth of Christ

> *"And an angel of the Lord appeared to them, and the glory of the Lord shone around them, and they were filled with great fear."*
>
> *Luke 2:9*

It was an ordinary night. Shepherds were quietly watching their flocks in the fields outside Bethlehem when heaven suddenly broke into the darkness. An angel of the Lord appeared, and the glory of the Lord shone all around them.

The night sky lit up with radiant light—brighter than any

star, moonlight, or campfire they had ever seen. Fear swept over them. But the angel's message was not one of judgment. It was pure good news: "Today in the city of David there has been born for you a Savior, who is Christ the Lord."

From a simple, everyday perspective, the shepherds witnessed an extraordinary burst of light. The darkness was suddenly filled with visible brightness—photons streaming out with an intensity far beyond anything natural. This wasn't fire like the burning bush. It wasn't a glow coming from a person's skin like Moses' face. This light came directly from the glory of the Lord, shining through His heavenly messenger.

Once again, we see the same pattern. In Genesis 1:3, God simply said, "Let there be light," and there was light. He didn't need fuel, fire, or any created thing—because He is the Creator of energy and light itself.

In the burning bush, God supplied divine energy that kept the plant shining without destroying it. On Mount Sinai, He caused Moses' face to radiate with His glory without harming him. Now, on this quiet hillside near Bethlehem, the glory of the Lord shone brightly around the shepherds. The light they saw wasn't produced by ordinary physical processes. The atoms and air around them were releasing visible photons, but the true source of that energy was the presence of God Himself.

This moment carries even deeper meaning. The light wasn't just a sign or a call. It announced that the Creator had stepped into His own creation. The eternal Son of God had taken on human flesh. The One through whom all things were made had entered the world He made.

The shepherds' fear made perfect sense. When God's glory touches our world, we instinctively know we are standing before something far greater than ourselves. Yet the angel's first words were, "Do not be afraid." This light wasn't meant to destroy them—it was meant to awaken them with joy. The Savior had come.

This is the fullest expression of the pattern we've been seeing. God reveals Himself through light again and again: at the burning bush, on Moses' face, and now at the birth of Christ. But here the light points to a Person. The glory shines because the Light of the world has arrived.

The same God whose fingerprints we will trace through quantum energy, motion, relativity, and even black holes is not distant from us. In Jesus, He has drawn near. The Creator entered our world of time, matter, and human struggle to redeem what sin had broken.

When God reveals Himself—whether through a burning bush, a radiant face, or the glory surrounding shepherds—He does it with purpose: to call us, to comfort us, and to draw us into relationship with Him. The question for every one of us is the same one the shepherds faced that night: Will we listen to the good news and come see this Savior for ourselves?

The Transfiguration of Christ

> *"His face shone like the sun, and his clothes became as white as the light."*
>
> *Matthew 17:1-4*

Jesus took Peter, James, and John up a high mountain.

There, right in front of them, something astonishing happened. Jesus was transfigured—His face began to shine with the brightness of the sun, and His clothes became dazzling white, glowing with pure light. Then Moses and Elijah appeared, talking with Him. In that moment, the Law and the Prophets stood alongside their fulfillment in Christ.

From a simple, everyday perspective, the disciples saw an overwhelming burst of light coming from Jesus Himself. This wasn't sunlight reflecting off His skin or clothes. It was radiant energy pouring out—photons streaming forth with the intensity of the sun. The light was so brilliant it would have been impossible for any human body to produce on its own.

This moment connects back to everything we've seen before. In Genesis 1:3, God simply said, "Let there be light," and there was light. He is the Creator of energy itself. In the burning bush, God supplied divine energy that kept the plant shining without consuming it. On Mount Sinai, He caused Moses' face to radiate with reflected glory without harming him. At Christ's birth, the glory of the Lord shone around the shepherds. Now, on this mountain, the light comes directly from Jesus—revealing who He truly is.

The Transfiguration wasn't just a spectacular display. It was a powerful revelation. For a brief time, the veil was pulled back, and the disciples glimpsed the divine glory that Jesus had with the Father before the world began (John 17:5). Moses and Elijah standing with Him showed that God's entire plan—from creation, through the Law and the Prophets—finds its perfect completion in Christ.

This encounter powerfully reinforces the consistent

pattern throughout Scripture: when God reveals Himself, light often accompanies the revelation. It is never random. It is a visible sign of His presence and authority.

The same God whose fingerprints we will trace through quantum energy, motion, relativity, and the extreme structures of black holes is the One who shone through Jesus on that mountain. In Christ, the Creator stepped into His creation not only to reveal His glory, but to redeem us.

When God reveals Himself—whether through a burning bush, a radiant face, the glory at His birth, or the dazzling light of the Transfiguration—He does so with purpose: to call us, to confirm who He is, and to draw us into deeper relationship with Him. The question for every one of us is the same one the disciples faced that day: Will we listen, believe, and worship the One whose light has come into our world?

The Resurrection of Christ

> *"His appearance was like lightning, and his clothing white as snow."*
>
> *Matthew 28:2-3*

Early on that first Easter morning, an angel descended from heaven along with a great earthquake. He rolled back the stone from Jesus' tomb, and the guards shook with fear. The angel's appearance was like lightning—bright, sudden, and overwhelming—and his clothing shone white as snow.

From a simple, everyday perspective, the scene was filled with intense, dazzling light. This wasn't ordinary sunlight or firelight. It was radiant energy pouring forth—

photons streaming out with the brilliant flash and purity of lightning, yet sustained and controlled. The light was so powerful it struck fear into the hardened Roman guards.

Yet this was no random burst of energy. The true source wasn't physical electricity or any created process. It came directly from the glory of God, announcing the greatest moment in history: Jesus had risen from the dead.

Once again, this light connects back to everything we've seen. In Genesis 1:3, God said, "Let there be light," and there was light. He is the Creator of energy itself. In the burning bush, God supplied divine energy that kept the plant shining without consuming it. On Mount Sinai, He caused Moses' face to radiate with His glory. At Jesus' birth, the glory of the Lord shone around the shepherds. On the Mount of Transfiguration, light poured from Jesus Himself, revealing His divine nature. Now, at the resurrection, that same divine light breaks through the darkness of the tomb.

The light at creation pushed back the formless darkness and began the story of the universe. The light at the resurrection pushes back the darkness of death and sin, beginning the story of new creation. No grave could hold the One who spoke light into existence. The same power that created the world now re-creates and redeems it.

The angel's radiant appearance was a visible declaration: death has been defeated. The Savior has conquered. The light that no darkness can overcome has triumphed.

This moment brings the pattern we've been tracing to its most powerful expression. Again and again, when God reveals Himself, light appears—not as a mere spectacle, but as a sign of His presence, authority, and redeeming love. The Creator who governs quantum energy, motion, relativity, and black holes is the same One who stepped into our broken world, conquered death, and now offers us new life.

When God reveals Himself—whether through a burning bush, a radiant face, the glory at Christ's birth, the Transfiguration, or the brilliant light of the resurrection—He does so with purpose: to call us out of darkness, to confirm His victory, and to draw us into eternal relationship with Him.

The question for every one of us is the same one the guards and the disciples faced that morning: Will we believe the good news that the Light has overcome the darkness?

Peter's Miraculous Escape from Prison

"And behold, an angel of the Lord stood next to him, and a light shone in the cell."

Acts 12:7-12

Peter was in prison, chained between two guards, with soldiers standing watch at the door. King Herod had already killed James, and Peter was next. But that night, everything changed. An angel of the Lord suddenly stood beside him, and a bright light filled the dark cell. Peter's chains fell off his wrists, the iron gate opened by itself, and he walked out a free man—still thinking at first that he was dreaming.

From a simple, everyday perspective, the prison cell was

suddenly flooded with light. There were no torches, no lamps, no natural source mentioned. Just light—bright enough to wake Peter and illuminate the entire space. This wasn't fire or reflected sunlight. It was radiant energy pouring into the darkness—photons streaming forth from the presence of the angel.

The same beautiful pattern continues. In Genesis 1:3, God said, "Let there be light," and there was light. He is the Creator of energy itself. In the burning bush, God supplied divine energy that kept the plant shining without consuming it. On Mount Sinai, He caused Moses' face to radiate with His glory. At Jesus' birth, the glory of the Lord shone around the shepherds. On the Mount of Transfiguration and at the resurrection, divine light broke through in overwhelming brilliance. Now, in this dark prison cell, the light of God's presence breaks in once more.

This light wasn't just for illumination. It was a sign of liberation. Peter's chains fell off. The gates opened. The darkness of bondage gave way to freedom. The same divine energy that created light at the beginning of the universe now reached into a man-made prison and set God's servant free—both physically and as a picture of the spiritual freedom Christ brings.

The light that filled that cell reminds us that no darkness is too deep for God. Whether it's the darkness of a prison, the darkness of doubt, or the darkness of sin, when God's glory shines, chains break and doors open.

This moment fits perfectly into the consistent pattern we've been tracing throughout Scripture: when God reveals Himself, light often appears—not as random spectacle, but as a visible sign of His presence, power, and rescuing love. The Creator who governs quantum energy, motion, relativity, and black holes is the same One who sends His light into the darkest places to set His people free.

When God reveals Himself—whether through a burning bush, a radiant face, the glory at Christ's birth, the Transfiguration, the resurrection, or a light in a prison cell—He does so with purpose: to call us, to deliver us, and to draw us into deeper relationship with Him.

The question for every one of us is the same one Peter faced that night: When the light breaks into our darkness, will we get up and follow?

Angelic Light Precedes Global Judgment

"The earth was made bright with his glory."

Revelation 18:1-2

In the dramatic vision given to John, an angel descends from heaven with great authority. As he comes, his glory lights up the entire earth. This is no small, localized glow like the light in Peter's prison cell or even the brilliance at Jesus' transfiguration. This light is global—bright enough to illuminate the whole planet.

From a simple, everyday perspective, imagine the night side of the earth suddenly becoming as bright as day. A flood of visible light—photons streaming out on a massive scale—

fills the world. There is no mention of scorching heat, destructive radiation, or harm to life. Just pure, overwhelming glory shining from the angel's presence.

The pattern by now is familiar. In Genesis 1:3, God simply said, "Let there be light," and there was light. He is the Creator of energy itself. In the burning bush, God supplied divine energy that kept the plant shining without consuming it. On Mount Sinai, Moses' face radiated with reflected glory. At Jesus' birth, the glory of the Lord shone around the shepherds. On the Mount of Transfiguration and at the resurrection, divine light broke through in power. In the prison cell, light brought freedom. Now, in this future moment, the light of God's glory fills the entire earth.

This global illumination is more than a spectacular sign. It announces that the time for final justice has come. Just as light at creation pushed back the darkness and brought order, this light dispels the darkness of evil and rebellion in preparation for God's righteous judgment. The same Creator who spoke light into existence at the beginning is the One who will one day flood the world with His glory.

The light that makes the whole earth bright reminds us that no darkness can ultimately stand against God. Whether it's personal darkness or the darkness covering the nations, when His glory shines, everything is exposed and His purposes move forward.

This moment brings the consistent biblical pattern to its fullest expression. Again and again, when God reveals Himself, light appears—not as random spectacle, but as a visible declaration of His presence, power, authority, and ultimate victory. The Creator who governs quantum energy, motion, relativity, and even black holes is the same One whose glory will one day light up the entire world.

When God reveals Himself—whether through a burning bush, a radiant face, the glory at Christ's birth, the Transfiguration, the resurrection, a light in a prison cell, or the global brightness before judgment—He does so with purpose: to call us, to deliver us, to warn us, and to draw us into eternal relationship with Him.

The question for every one of us is this: When we see the light of His presence breaking into our world, will we turn toward it—or turn away?

The Power That Changes a Life

From the burning bush to the empty tomb, the pattern is unmistakable.

God reveals Himself through light.
Man responds.
History changes.

Every one of those moments carried a purpose:

Moses was called.
The shepherds received good news.
Peter walked free.
The world was warned.

But the greatest miracle is not that God can make a bush burn without being consumed, or cause a face to shine, or flood a prison cell with light.

The greatest miracle is that He can do the same thing inside a human heart.

When a person hears the call of God and responds in faith, the same Creator who once said "Let there be light" now speaks into a soul—and light breaks in again. The Holy Spirit comes. Chains fall. A new creation begins.

This is no mere self-improvement.

This is re-creation.

The resurrection was not just proof that God can raise the dead.

It was the opening of a door—so that the same power that raised Jesus can now raise you.

Part 1 has shown us this foundation:

> God defines reality.
> You are created in His image.
> His Word is reliable.
> And when He reveals Himself, He does it with purpose—*to redeem and to restore relationship with you.*

Now we turn to Part 2.

Because the God who speaks light into a human soul is the very same God who structured the cosmos. The power that changes a life is the power that holds the universe together.

And that power is worth knowing more deeply.

Chapter 6: Summary

This chapter answers a deeper question: *Why does God reveal Himself at all?*

From the burning bush to the empty tomb—and even into the future—God repeatedly steps into our world through light. Each appearance carries clear purpose: to call, to confirm, to rescue, to warn, and to redeem. The light is never random. It is a visible sign of His presence and authority. In every case, the atoms and molecules simply release the photons we can see, while the true source of energy is God Himself—the same Creator who first said, "Let there be light."

Yet all these spectacular moments point to something even greater. The ultimate miracle is not what God does in bushes, faces, or prison cells. It is what He does inside a human heart. When a person hears His call and responds in faith, the same power that raised Jesus from the dead and sustains the universe now brings new life. Chains fall. A new creation begins.

Part 1 has laid a solid foundation: God defines reality, we are created in His image, His Word is reliable, and He reveals Himself with purpose. That purpose is not merely to be observed, but to be known personally.

Now we turn to Part 2. Because the God who speaks light into a human soul is the very same God who structured the cosmos. The power that changes a life is the power that holds the universe together.

And that power is worth knowing more deeply.

PART 2
The Science

7 — The Building Block of Creation

"The actual point of creation lies outside the scope of presently known laws of physics." [23]

Stephen Hawking, the Big Bang, and God

Dr. Henry F. Schaefer III

Stephen Hawking acknowledged that the actual point of creation lies outside the scope of presently known laws of physics. In other words, the beginning of the universe is not something physics can fully explain from within its own system.

That admission stands in quiet harmony with the opening words of Genesis: "Let there be light." Scripture does not begin with matter. It begins with light. To understand creation, we must begin where God began—with

---

[23] Henry F. Schaefer III. Center for Computational Quantum Chemistry. University of Georgia Athens, Georgia. *Stephen Hawking, the Big Bang, and God.* 2004 New College Lecture Series. (2004) https://newcollege.unsw.edu.au/downloads/File/pdf/Lectures_Summaries/The%20Big%20Bang.pdf

the first physical act recorded in Scripture.

Why Understanding Energy Matters

> *"God blessed them and said to them, 'Be fruitful and multiply! Fill the earth and subdue it! Rule over the fish of the sea and the birds of the air and every creature that moves on the ground.'"*
>
> *Genesis 1:28 NET*

Understanding energy is vital for grasping both the universe and our role as stewards of God's creation. Einstein's equation $E=mc^2$ reveals that everything, including us, is a form of concentrated energy. The Sun's energy sustains life, drives weather, and powers ecosystems, emphasizing our dependence on this divine provision.[24]

Recognizing energy's central role helps us make informed decisions about the environment, health, and technology. Yet our knowledge of quantum energy remains primitive, as seen in trial-and-error approaches prevalent in medicine and cancer treatment. By better understanding energy, we align with our God-given responsibility to care for His creation and improve our quality of life.

What Is Meant by Quantum Energy

In this book the simple phrase *quantum energy* is used to describe how light—God's first creation—behaves at the

---

[24] Haigh, Joanna, Professor Imperial College of London. Climate Assembly UK. https://www.climateassembly.uk/about/meetings/january-24/professor-joanna-haigh-imperial-college-london-what-climate-change/index.html

smallest scales. Physicists study this through *quantum mechanics*, and more specifically through *quantum electrodynamics (QED)* when light interacts with matter.[25]

The key idea is this: energy doesn't flow in a continuous stream. It flows in packets. A packet of light is a photon. Photons trade energy with matter in precise, step-like amounts.

Think of them as **raindrops**. Sometimes they fall gently, like sunlight warming your skin. At other times they are like hail—exerting a destructive force such as a laser light that can burn through paper. And sometimes, when countless drops arrive together, they create ripples and patterns we don't expect.

> *"For with You is the fountain of life; in Your light we see light."*
>
> *Psalm 36:9, NASB*

A World Painted by Light

"Light" isn't only what our eyes see. The electromagnetic spectrum runs from high-energy gamma rays and X-rays, through ultraviolet and visible light, down to infrared, microwaves, and radio waves.

Higher energy → shorter wavelength;
Lower energy → longer wavelength.[26]

---

[25] Richard P. Feynman, QED, the strange theory of light and matter. 2006 by Princeton University Press. Page 6.

[26] NASA. *Electromagnetic Spectrum Diagram*. (June 2023). https://mynasadata.larc.nasa.gov/basic-page/electromagnetic-spectrum-diagram

Some photons heal (infrared warmth).
Some reveal (X-rays in medicine).
Some harm (ultraviolet on skin).

All day long your body trades these raindrops with the world—absorbing, emitting, reflecting.

In a very real sense, you are a **quantum energy container** living in a quantum world. Made of the same stuff God made when He said, "Let there be light."

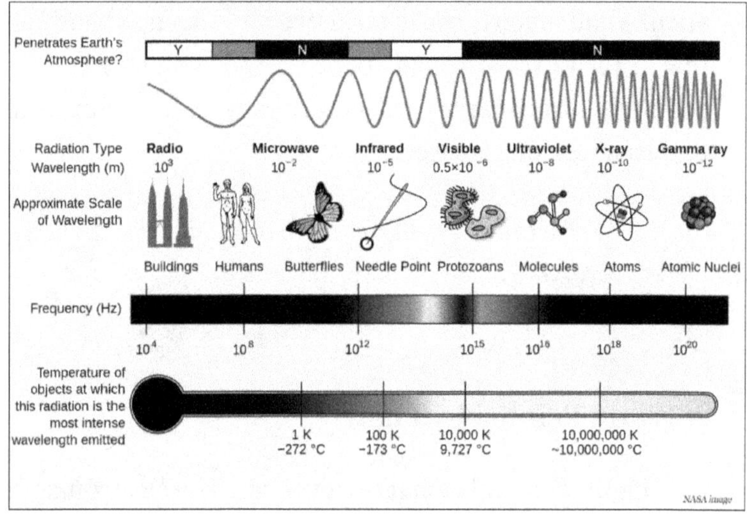

The Quantum Raindrop

> *"What is the way to the abode of light? And where does darkness reside?"*
>
> *Job 38:24 (NIV)*

Close your eyes for a moment and picture a summer shower. Each raindrop falls separately—distinct, whole, and refreshing—yet together they create something far greater:

the gentle pitter-patter on leaves, the splashes on the ground, the life-giving water soaks into the earth—and the ability for a gentle shower to turn into a fierce storm.

Centuries ago, Isaac Newton looked at light with that same sense of wonder. Passing sunlight through a prism, he watched white light split into a rainbow and concluded that light must be made of tiny particles, or "corpuscles." Each color, he believed, was carried by its own indivisible little bundle. It was a revolutionary idea for its time—light as something solid and real, not just something that pierces the darkness.

Then, in the twentieth century, Dr. Richard Feynman invited us to look again, this time through the startling lens of quantum physics. Where Newton saw rigid corpuscles, Feynman saw something more alive and playful: light as a shower of quantum "*raindrops*".

In his famous lectures on quantum electrodynamics (QED), Feynman described photons—the particles of light—as individual droplets. "Light is something like raindrops," he said. "Each little lump of light is called a photon, and if the light is all one color, all the raindrops are the same size."

He knew this would surprise many of us. After all, most of us grew up hearing that light behaves like waves—smooth, flowing ripples on a pond. Feynman gently but firmly corrected the picture:

> *"I want to emphasize that light comes in this form, particles. It is very important to know that light behaves like particles, especially for those of you who have gone to school, where you were probably told something about light behaving like*

waves. I'm telling you the way it does behave, like particles."[27]

Dr. Richard Feynman, QED

His raindrop metaphor is more than clever wording—it is clarity. It helps us feel the quantum world instead of just thinking about it.

Light arrives not as a continuous stream, but as countless separate photons, each one a tiny packet of energy with its own properties. One photon strikes a leaf and helps power photosynthesis. Another enters your eye and becomes the color blue in a child's drawing. Each is discrete. Each is real.

In this way, Feynman's quantum raindrop becomes a bridge. It honors Newton's insight while carrying us deeper—into a realm where light is both particle and mystery, governed by laws more elegant and surprising than either scientist could have fully imagined. Laws, we might say, woven by the Creator of that summer shower and the rainbow alike.

Quantum Energy Interaction

"He reveals mysteries from the darkness And brings the deep darkness into light."

Job 12:22 (NASB)

Imagine stepping onto a quiet basketball court with a friend. You bounce the ball, and it behaves exactly as you

---

[27] ibid. 15.

expect—predictable, solid, following the straightforward rules of everyday physics. Aim it one way, and it goes that way. Your friend catches it without mystery.

Now flip the lights off and place a single sheet of white paper on the floor. Switch on a flashlight. The paper glows softly. But here's what feels almost magical: your friend standing in front of the paper sees it clearly... and so does everyone else in the darkened gym—even those standing behind you.

The photons pouring from your flashlight don't behave like that basketball. They don't simply travel in a straight line and stop. When they strike the paper, they scatter in every direction at once. That humble sheet of paper sends quantum raindrops in every direction so that anyone who looks can see its glow.

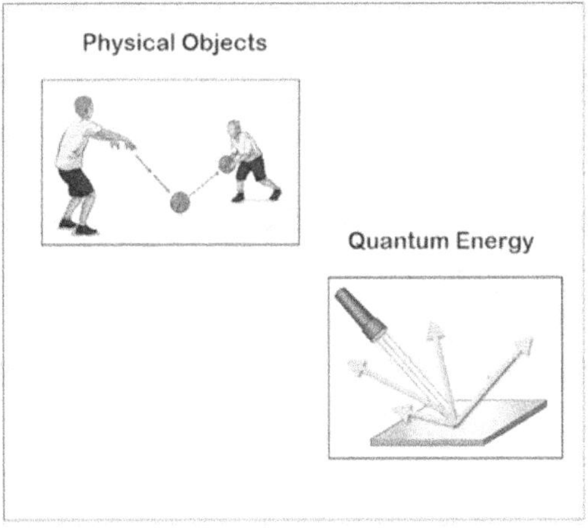

This is where the mystery deepens. Those photons don't just bounce off the surface like rubber balls. They interact with the very atoms that make up the paper. Each tiny packet of light engages with the electrons inside those atoms, exciting them and triggering a cascade of new photons that spread everywhere—even back toward you, the one holding the flashlight. What looks like simple reflection is actually a profound conversation happening at the quantum level between energy and matter.

You can feel the reality of this interaction every day. Step outside on a sunny afternoon. The warmth on your skin is not just "sunshine"—it is countless photons delivering their energy to the molecules in your body. Stay too long, and that same gentle energy can turn into a sunburn, a visible reminder of how deeply light penetrates and transforms the matter it touches.

Turn up the intensity even further and the transformation becomes dramatic. Shine a high-powered laser on that same sheet of paper. The photons slam into the atoms with such force that electrons vibrate violently, chemical bonds break, and the paper bursts into flame. What began as quiet illumination becomes powerful change—all because of quantum energy interaction.

Even something as ordinary as color tells this story. A red sheet of paper absorbs most wavelengths of light but reflects the red ones. Those reflected photons reach your eyes, stimulate the receptors in your retina, and your brain instantly translates them into the experience of "red." A mirror does something similar but with precise angles, letting you see your own reflection because the photons obey consistent, orderly rules.

This is the beauty of the quantum raindrop. In our everyday world, a basketball follows simple, predictable paths. But light—those tiny, discrete packets Feynman described—operates on a deeper, more intimate level. Every photon is a messenger, not merely illuminating the world but revealing how energy and matter dance together in ways classical physics could never fully explain.

And in that dance, we catch a glimpse of something even more wonderful. The same God who spoke light into existence designed these interactions with exquisite care. He didn't create a cold, mechanical universe. He made one alive with mystery and order, where even the smallest particles of light whisper of a Creator whose works are deeper, stranger, and more beautiful than we could ever imagine on our own.

Quantum Interference

To grasp the deeper mysteries of quantum energy, we must turn our attention to a concept both fascinating and perplexing: *constructive* and *destructive interference.*

Imagine standing by a still pond and tossing two stones into the water. The ripples spread outward. As they move, they meet other ripples, and at these points of contact, something remarkable happens. In some places, the waves combine and grow stronger, producing larger ripples—this is *constructive interference.* In other places, the waves cancel each other out, leaving the surface calm—this is *destructive interference.*

Now, transport this simple idea into the quantum world. Here, particles—whether electrons, photons, or others—are not merely dots in space. Like the ripples in the pond, they move through space with wave-like behavior, and when they meet, they do not merely pass by unaffected. Instead, they interfere with one another. In some instances, they amplify each other's effects through constructive interference. In others, they cancel each other out through destructive interference. This interaction is at the heart of quantum mechanics, revealing that particles are more than solitary entities—they are part of a dynamic, ever-changing interaction.

Take the case of light. When light passes through a narrow slit, or through several slits, it does not travel in a straight line as one might expect. Instead, the particles of light—photons—interfere with one another, creating patterns of light and shadow on a surface.[28] Where the light waves strengthen each other, bright areas appear, the result of constructive interference. Where they cancel each other, dark areas emerge, marking the places where destructive interference has taken hold.[29] These patterns reveal the dual nature of light, for it behaves not only as particles but also as waves, shifting between both in ways that challenge common thinking.

Consider now the behavior of an electron, that most elusive of particles. We might imagine it as a point orbiting the nucleus of an atom, but in the quantum world, it behaves more like a wave—spread out, interacting with itself and with other particles. The electron's position is not fixed, but shaped by interference patterns, determined by where constructive and destructive forces allow it to exist. This is

---

[28] David J. Griffiths. *Introduction to Quantum Mechanics.* Quantum Scattering Theory, pg. 379. Cambridge University Press; 3rd edition (August 16, 2018)

[29] Anil Ananthaswamy. Nature. *Particle, wave, both or neither? The experiment that challenges all we know about reality.* June 13, 2023. https://www.nature.com/articles/d41586-023-01938-6

not randomness, but a delicate interplay of forces that create a probability, a likely place for the electron to be found, but never a certainty.

The quantum world, then, is one of interaction and interference, where even the smallest particles do not stand alone. Constructive and destructive interference are not mere abstractions—they are the very principles that govern how energy behaves, how light moves, and how matter itself is shaped. Beneath the surface of the reality we perceive lies a deeper, richer world, where particles and waves are constantly affecting one another in ways that are, to our minds, both unexpected and wondrous.

Quantum Entanglement

> *"Am I only a God nearby," declares the Lord, "and not a God far away? Who can hide in secret places so that I cannot see them?" declares the Lord. "Do not I fill heaven and earth?"*
>
> *Jeremiah 23:23-24 (NIV)*

Quantum entanglement offers us a glimpse, however faint, of the omnipresence of God. Among the many mysteries of quantum energy, entanglement stands as one of the most profound.

When two subatomic particles become entangled, their very essence becomes intertwined in such a way that the state of one instantly affects the other—no matter how far apart they may be. In this, we see an echo of God's own nature—His presence and influence pervading all things, everywhere, at once.

Picture, if you will, two magical coins. You flip one, it lands on heads, and the other flips to tails. Nobody has touched the second coin. No wires or mechanisms are seen. It seems to have a life of its own and knows when the other coin is flipped and whether it is heads or tails. It seems to happen by magic.

Curious, you separate the coins by an immense distance—miles, perhaps even light years apart—yet the magic remains. As soon as you flip the first coin again, the other responds, turning to the opposite side in perfect synchrony. This, strange as it may seem, is a shadow of the mysterious behavior we observe in "quantum entanglement".

Scientists, in their quest to unravel the mysteries of this phenomenon, use lasers to entangle pairs of ions—small particles of matter. Once entangled, these particles are separated, often by great distances. Each ion possesses a spin state, which, for the sake of simplicity, can be likened to the heads or tails of a coin. Here is where it becomes truly fascinating: if one ion's spin is altered, the spin of the other changes instantly, regardless of the distance between them.

In our ordinary, everyday world, we expect such interactions to require some form of physical connection—a string, a gravitational pull, an electromagnetic wave. Yet, in the quantum realm, no such tether exists. This immediate influence between two particles separated by vast distances defies the limits of our intuition. It challenges the very fabric of how we understand space and time.

Albert Einstein, with characteristic wit, dubbed this "spooky action at a distance," a term that aptly captures both the wonder and the discomfort such a discovery brings. For how can two particles, so far apart, communicate instantaneously? Even now, we grapple with this question, as we seek to unlock the deeper, more intricate workings of the quantum world—an unseen universe that behaves in ways that are, to our minds, both baffling and profound.

Quantum Superposition

Consider turning on a TV, only to discover something astonishing: instead of showing just one channel, the screen simultaneously displays every channel at once. Sports, news, sitcoms, and cooking shows are all jumbled together in a swirling mosaic. It's only when you sit down, pick up the remote, and focus your gaze on the screen that the chaos fades, and one channel—just one—comes into clear view.

This idea might sound impossible, but in the world of quantum physics, something very much like this actually happens. Welcome to the strange and fascinating concept of *superposition.*

What is superposition? In our everyday world, objects exist in definite states. A coin in your hand, for instance, is either heads or tails—never both. A TV, whether turned on or off, is tuned to just one channel at a time.

But in the quantum realm, the rules are entirely different. Subatomic particles like electrons and photons don't settle for "either-or." Instead, they exist in a state of superposition, meaning they occupy multiple states simultaneously. It's as if a quantum TV doesn't commit to one channel but plays them all at once—until, that is, someone observes it.

This idea resonates with the biblical concept that some aspects of creation are "unfathomable" to human understanding. As Romans 11:33 (NASB) reminds us, "Oh, the depth of the riches, both of the wisdom and knowledge of God! How unsearchable are His judgments and unfathomable His ways!" The quantum world, with its layers of mystery, hints at a Creator whose wisdom far surpasses human comprehension.

Why does observation matter? Here's where things get strange: the moment you look at a quantum system, it "chooses" a single state, collapsing from superposition into something definite. For our quantum TV, this means turning it on and observing the screen forces it to display one channel, seemingly at random.

Before you look, the system exists in a kind of limbo, embodying every possibility at the same time. Observation is what gives it a concrete reality, just as tuning into one channel ends the TV's many-channel *superposition*.

This invites a reflection on the unseen nature of reality. As Hebrews 11:1 (NASB) states, "Now faith is the certainty of things hoped for, a proof of things not seen." Just as the quantum world operates on principles we cannot fully see or grasp, so faith challenges us to trust in what lies beyond our immediate perception.

Superposition might sound like a quirky idea, but it's absolutely essential to one of today's most exciting technologies: quantum computing.

While classical computers process information step by step—like flipping through TV channels one at a time—

quantum computers take a radically different approach. Thanks to superposition, they can explore multiple possibilities at once, like our quantum TV showing every channel simultaneously.

This ability allows quantum computers to solve problems that are far too complex for classical computers to handle in a reasonable time. Whether it's discovering new medicines, solving intricate puzzles in logistics, or tackling advanced AI challenges, superposition gives quantum computers their extraordinary power.

Why does it matter? Superposition isn't just an abstract concept; it's a glimpse into a universe that is far more mysterious and wondrous than we often realize. It challenges our classical notions of reality and serves as the foundation for technologies that have the potential to reshape our future.

As Romans 11:33 and Hebrews 11:1 emphasize, the mysteries of the quantum world point us toward a Creator whose wisdom and creation surpass our understanding. For believers, superposition becomes more than just a scientific curiosity; it is a reason to marvel at the beauty and complexity of God's work.

These verses highlight God's sovereignty, the mystery of creation, and the unseen aspects of reality. While superposition may not directly relate to biblical teachings, it provides an opportunity to appreciate the intricacies of creation and the One who designed it. For believers, such mysteries serve as a reminder of the depth of God's wisdom and the beauty of a universe that reflects His glory.

Photon Multiplication

Quantum energy is indeed mysterious but isn't confined to the laboratory, it's also making waves on the battlefield, pun intended.

Night vision technology is a good example of the practical application of quantum energy; often used by special operators like Navy SEALs. Night vision goggles, often referred to as NVGs, rely on something called photon multiplication.

When a single photon strikes the charged plate in a night-vision device, it triggers a cascade of electrons that multiplies the signal thousands of times. That tiny spark becomes bright enough to form a clear image—allowing operators to see in near-total darkness.[30]

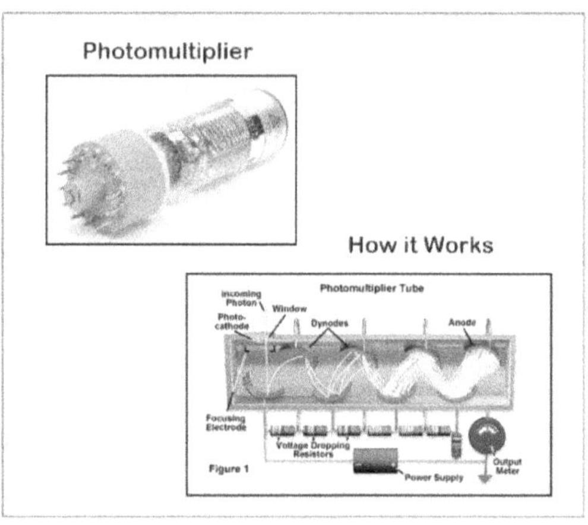

This practical application of quantum energy highlights how cutting-edge scientific principles can be harnessed to

[30] Image source: Florida State University. Hamamatsu Learning Center. accessed September 5, 2023, http://hamamatsu.magnet.fsu.edu/articles/photomultipliers.html

significantly enhance real-world capabilities. By leveraging the unique properties of quantum mechanics, such as the ability to detect and amplify even the faintest light and heat signatures, technologies like night vision goggles give users an unparalleled advantage in complex and challenging environments.

But the implications go far beyond military use. The same principles that allow SEALs to navigate treacherous terrain under the cover of night are being explored in various fields—from improving medical imaging techniques to developing more efficient solar panels that can capture and convert energy even in low-light conditions.

This ability to translate abstract quantum theories into practical tools and solutions not only revolutionizes specific industries but also pushes the boundaries of what we consider possible, opening up new frontiers for innovation and discovery in the 21st century.

You Already Depend on Quantum Energy

You may never think about quantum raindrops while you're driving to work, checking your phone, or sitting in a doctor's office—but you are relying on them every single moment.

When you use GPS on your phone, you are trusting the precise timing of signals that must be corrected for the relativistic effects of quantum energy and gravity. Without those tiny adjustments rooted in the behavior of light, your map would be off by miles within minutes.

The same quantum principles that make your phone's

clock accurate also make the internet secure through quantum communication techniques that detect any attempt to eavesdrop.

Walk outside on a cold winter morning and feel the warmth of the sun on your face—that is quantum energy at work, the same packets of light God first spoke into existence.

Your solar-powered calculator, the panels on rooftops, even the latest perovskite solar cells in research labs, all depend on understanding how those photons interact with matter at the quantum level.

Step into a hospital for an MRI or a PET scan and you are seeing quantum energy in action again—photons and positrons revealing what no ordinary light could show.

Night-vision goggles used by soldiers, the lasers that perform delicate eye surgery, the quantum sensors in your car's anti-lock brakes—all trace their power back to the same foundational reality: light behaving as discrete, interactive packets.

You don't have to understand the math to depend on it. Every time you flip a light switch, look at a digital display, or trust a medical image, you are living inside the world God began with the words "Let there be light."

Why Start Here?

Why start here? Because everything else in Part 2, The Science, builds on it. Black holes—those mysterious regions in space where gravity is so strong even light can't escape—are not exceptions to God's order; they are extreme examples where His first building block is pushed to its limits. To understand why time stretches near a black hole, why stars shine, or why sunlight warms your skin even in winter, we must begin where God began: "Let there be light."

God's Eternal Nature and the Creation of Time

> *"For the LORD gives wisdom, and from his mouth comes knowledge and understanding."*
>
> *Proverbs 2:6 NET*

Judeo-Christian Scripture teaches that God transcends time and is eternal. However, there are those in modern society who would scoff at that idea, calling it a fairy tale or mythology. But they cannot scoff at the indisputable fact that black holes and GPS satellites are examples in our world where time does not behave in a way that we expect. Time approaches infinity in black holes, and GPS Satellite time is different from time on the surface of the earth.

Time is intrinsically woven into quantum energy. When God said, "Let there be light," He simultaneously created both quantum energy and our concept of time, which we will discuss in later chapters. But His creation of quantum energy wasn't just limited to time; it's also connected to the motion of the planets, the existence of black holes, and miracles in the Bible, like the Burning Bush and the transfiguration of Christ. They're all connected.

The eternal nature of God is beautifully expressed in Romans 1:20 (NASB): "For since the creation of the world His invisible attributes, His eternal power and divine nature, have been clearly seen, being understood through what has been made, so that they are without excuse." Scripture links His eternal power and divine nature to His creation. So, shouldn't we pay special attention to the first thing he created - light?

The Building Block of Creation

We began this chapter with the assertion: physics cannot step outside itself to explain why the universe, or anything it contains, including us, exists at all.

Even our most brilliant minds admit that the actual point of creation lies beyond presently known laws.

Scripture does not hesitate at that boundary. It simply declares, "Let there be light."

What this chapter has shown is that light placed at the opening of Genesis is structural. At the smallest scales of reality, energy does not drift aimlessly. It arrives in packets. It interacts with matter precisely. It forms patterns through interference. It connects distant particles in ways that challenge intuition. It carries multiple possibilities until a measurable outcome emerges.

The world you experience each day is a result of the first act of creation.

When you step into sunlight, you are not merely standing in brightness. You are standing in a continual cascade of quantum events. When you see your reflection in a mirror, photons are tracing exact angles. When a laser cuts steel or a sensor detects faint radiation from deep space, it is the same foundational reality at work. The first physical act recorded in Scripture continues to sustain and structure everything that followed.

Light is not only what allows us to see. It is part of what makes seeing possible at all.

And if light is foundational—if it is woven into matter, motion, measurement, and time—then the rest of creation must be understood in relation to it. Black holes, gravitational curvature, and the stretching of time are not departures from this order; they are its extreme expressions. The same building block spoken into existence at the beginning is present when gravity bends spacetime and when stars exhaust their fuel.

Genesis begins with light because light is not incidental.

It is the first layer of physical structure.

And once we recognize that, we are no longer looking at an ancient sentence. We are looking at the opening act in a universe whose depth we are only beginning to understand.

Chapter 7: Summary

This chapter marks a transition—from understanding who God is to understanding how His creation works.

It begins with a simple but profound idea: if God created the universe, then the first act of creation matters. Scripture begins with light, and science reveals that light—energy—is not just part of the universe, but is foundational to it.

At the smallest scales, energy does not flow randomly. It moves in precise, measurable packets, interacts with matter, and shapes everything we experience—from the warmth of the sun to the structure of atoms. What appears simple on the surface is built on a deeper, more complex reality.

This chapter introduces that deeper layer. Concepts like photon interaction, interference, entanglement, and superposition reveal a world that does not behave according to everyday intuition. Yet these same principles are not abstract—they are at work in real life, shaping technology, medicine, and our understanding of the universe.

The point is not simply to explain quantum mechanics. It is to show that the physical world reflects order, precision, and structure at its foundation. The same light spoken into existence at the beginning continues to sustain and govern everything that follows.

In the end, this chapter establishes a starting point for Part 2: to understand the universe, we must begin where God began.

With light.

8 — Energy Cannot be Created

"Then God said, 'Let there be light'; and there was light."

Genesis 1:3

If everything in the universe is ultimately made from energy—the very stuff God spoke into existence with 'Let there be light'—then an obvious question follows: How does this energy actually behave within the ordered creation He sustains? Does it act randomly, or does it reveal the same boundaries and reliability we see throughout Scripture?

We Cannot Create Energy

Did you know that we can't *create* energy? Only God can. However, we can transform energy by converting it from one form into another.

The First Law of Thermodynamics states that energy cannot be created or destroyed. You might imagine the universe as an enormous snow globe—everything inside keeps moving, but nothing new enters or leaves; it all stays within the glass. Plants grow; plants die. Animals are born, then perish. The cycle of life is more than a scientific reality; it is part of God's plan.

Let's zoom in on the idea of "generating" energy. Think about a coal power plant. It doesn't *create* energy from nothing; instead, it *transforms* the energy stored in coal into heat and electrical energy. The First Law of Thermodynamics shows this process follows the physics rulebook.

All of the energy in the universe, in the form of stars, planets, plants and animals, is exactly the same as the moment the universe was created. The energy we see in the universe today didn't come from within itself, it came from God, who exists beyond it.

The very power that drives everything around us wasn't a random occurrence or something that always existed on its own. It was intentionally brought into existence by a Creator who operates outside the physical limits of the universe. All that energy - everything we see, feel, and use—started with God's command.

God's Infinite Energy

> *"Through him all things were made; without him nothing was made that has been made. In him was life, and that life was the light of all mankind.*
>
> *John 1:3-4 (NIV)*

Picture yourself stepping into a dark room and turning on a light. Instantly, a humble 60-watt incandescent bulb begins its work, emitting photons—billions upon billions of them. In fact, that little light produces around 33 quintillion photons each second.

The mind struggles to grasp such a number, so let me give you a sense of its scale: If someone promised you an answer in a million seconds, you'd wait about 11 and a half days. A billion seconds? That's just over 31 years. But a trillion seconds—well, you'd be waiting over 31,000 years. Now imagine waiting a *quintillion* seconds—it's nearly beyond comprehension. Yet, that's the number of photons your lightbulb sends out each second, a staggering reminder of the vast complexity even in the simplest things we take for granted.

- 1 million seconds = 11.6 days
- 1 billion seconds = 31.7 years
- 1 trillion seconds = 31,709.8 years
- 1 quintillion seconds = 31,709,791,983.76 years

Perhaps you've never given it much thought, but mathematics is invaluable at explaining the invisible. So, let's give it a try. Our 60-watt incandescent light bulb works diligently but, at only about 2% efficiency, most of its energy goes to waste as heat. That leaves around 1.2 joules of energy per second going into producing light. Let's assume the average wavelength of this light is around 550 nanometers - right in the sweet spot of visible light.

Using Planck's equation, we find that each photon, each little packet of light, carries about 3.6×10^{-19} joules of energy.[31] The number of photons this bulb pumps out in just one second? An astounding 33 quintillion, or 33,000,000,000,000,000,000! Our humble incandescent lightbulb is producing more photons in one second than you could count in several lifetimes.

Stop and think about this for a minute:

> *Since energy can neither be created nor destroyed, all of the energy currently in the universe came into being at the moment the universe was created.*

We live in a **closed system** whose total energy has **remained constant** since God created it in the beginning.

If a light bulb can generate an immense number of photons every second, it is almost beyond comprehension how much energy was brought into existence at the moment of creation. The creation of the universe stands as a profound testimony to God's infinite power.

Generating Quantum Energy

A photon (quantum energy) is generated by transforming heat into a photon light, but how does that happen?

When an iron plate is heated, the electrons start leaping from their ***ground state*** to higher energy levels, or an ***excited state***, not unlike popcorn kernels bursting in a hot

---

[31] Panfil, Miłosz, PhD. "Photon Energy Calculator", OMNI Calculator, (7/29/2024). https://www.omnicalculator.com/physics/photon-energy

pan.

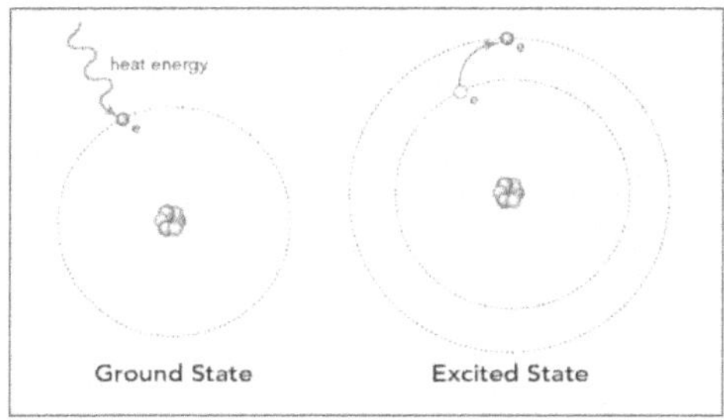

At first, the iron plate glows orange because the electrons aren't venturing very far from their original orbit and the light looks red or orange, the lower end of the visible light spectrum. But if we keep adding heat, the color changes until it becomes white hot, not unlike an electric bulb. The electrons are jumping to higher levels and releasing photons whose frequencies cover the full spectrum of visible light.

However, the iron atom electrons are *unstable* as they travel to higher levels. Seeking stability, they return to their "*ground state.*" But they can't return unless they release energy in the form of photons of light, quantum raindrops.

Every bit of light we see, whether it is from a star or an electric bulb, is the result of an electron shedding some of its energy and returning to a stable state.

Each photon of light in the universe is produced by the same process. This is an important concept. Whether it blazes forth from the Sun, dances in the flicker of a fireplace, or glows faintly from the metabolic reactions in your own body, it all follows the same fundamental rule: an excited electron must give up energy to return to stability, and it does so by releasing a photon—generating, not creating, light—a process of transformation from one form to another.

This single, elegant mechanism spans every corner of creation, from the most distant stars to the warmth of your own skin, linking the vast and the intimate in one continuous story. It is a wonderful system of balance—the universe itself upholding God's perfect order. By observing this process, we take a step closer to understanding not only the mechanics of quantum energy but also the deeper truths that govern our world.

The Interchangeability of Mass and Energy

Our bodies are constantly engaging in an intricate exchange of quantum energy with our surroundings.[32] We are living, breathing repositories of God's first creation.[33] Einstein's equation $E=mc^2$ demonstrates that mass and energy are interchangeable, and by understanding this relationship we see how God's creation is both scientifically profound and spiritually meaningful.

---

[32] Unglaub. Dee. "Human Physiology: An Integrated Approach 8th Edition". Energy and cellular metabolism. Pg. 92. Pearson; 8th edition (January 3, 2018)

[33] Stanfield. Cindy L. "Principles of Human Physiology". Cell metabolism. Pearson; 6th edition (January 5, 2016)

Quantum Energy Defies the Predictable and Measurable

Even though matter is essentially concentrated energy, matter and energy exhibit contrasting behaviors.[34] Physical matter, like your car, can change speed (velocity). But a photon of light? It's a different story. It races through the universe at an unwavering speed of 186,000 miles per second in a vacuum. No revving up, no slowing down; it's as if it's always on cruise control.

Think about the light emanating from stars that are trillions of miles away. When you gaze at a star, you're not witnessing the star itself. You're seeing the quantum energy it produces.

Light is a traveler that maintains its relentless pace as it meets your eye and interacts with your retina and optic nerve, revealing the existence of distant planets and stars. In essence, your eyes are connected to the quantum energy which began in a distant galaxy.

Prior to the 1940's, many scientists found quantum behavior to be quite chaotic and perplexing. The initial discoveries in quantum mechanics were so counterintuitive compared to classical mechanics that they appeared almost chaotic in nature, not something produced by an orderly God who created the universe.

By the late 1940s and early 1950s, Dr. Richard Feynman introduced diagrams that provided a visual and

---

[34] Einstein, Albert. "The Meaning of Relativity: Including the Relativistic Theory of the Non-Symmetric Field - Fifth Edition". Princeton Science Library, 32, 5th Edition

calculational tool to represent and simplify interactions between quantum particles.[35] This transformed the idea of chaotic and complex quantum electrodynamics into an orderly framework.

These diagrams also helped to intuitively grasp the processes happening at the quantum level, thereby reducing the perception of chaos and bringing a sense of order to quantum mechanics.

The journey from the early chaotic perceptions of quantum mechanics to the structured understanding provided by Feynman's diagrams highlights the progression of our comprehension of the universe. As we gain a deeper appreciation for the order and elegance underlying the fundamental forces of nature, we also gain a deeper appreciation for the Creator.

Energy Cannot Be Created

We struggle to comprehend a quintillion photons per second from a single light bulb.

Thirty-three quintillion.
From something you hold in your hand.

Now step back.

That same physical law applies to the Sun—only on a scale so large that it radiates more energy in one second than humanity has used in all of history.

---

[35] Richard P. Feynman, QED, the strange theory of light and matter. 2006 by Princeton University Press. Page 27.

And the Sun is an average star.

There are hundreds of billions of stars in our galaxy alone.

There are hundreds of billions of galaxies.

Every one of them radiating energy.
Every second.
Without interruption.

All of that energy—every photon ever emitted, every nuclear reaction ever ignited, every spark in every star—was present in potential at the beginning.

Energy cannot create itself.

It cannot emerge from nothing inside the system.

So at some moment outside the system, all of it had to be brought into existence.

Not partially.
Not gradually.
Not experimentally.

Completely.

The total energy contained in the universe—from the brightest quasar to the faintest ember—had to be spoken into existence in one sovereign act.

Try to imagine that.

Every sunrise you have ever seen.
Every bolt of lightning.

Every flame.
Every heartbeat.

Every thought formed by electrical impulses in your brain.

All of it is the result of that first act.

The universe is not generating power—transforming it.

And it has been transforming it for thousands of years.

Yet the total remains conserved, exactly as physics predicts.

The First Law of Thermodynamics does not diminish God's power—it magnifies it. It tells us that the energy we see today did not arise from within the universe. It was endowed.

Creation was not merely the shaping of matter.

It was the creation of energy on a scale beyond imagination.

This is not abstract theology.

You are alive because of that act.

The warmth in your body.
The electrical impulses in your nervous system.
The light entering your eyes as you read this page.

You are sustained by the same energy that began when God said, "Let there be light."

And here is the overwhelming reality:

If the total energy of the universe had to be brought into existence at once—then the One who did it is not merely powerful.

He is without limit.

Not measured in watts.
Not measured in joules.
Not measured in mass.

Infinite.

The incandescent bulb humbles us.
The stars stagger us.
The galaxies silence us.

But they are not the source.

They are evidence.

Energy cannot be created—yet it is.

Created by the Great I AM.

Pause there.

Everything you have ever touched, every sunrise you have witnessed, every breath you have taken, every electrical impulse that allowed you to form a single thought—all of it exists because, at some moment outside the system, God created the universe with its total energy.

You are not observing that power from a distance.

You are living inside it.

Chapter 8: Summary

This chapter takes a simple principle of physics and follows it to its unavoidable conclusion: energy cannot create itself.

The First Law of Thermodynamics tells us that energy can be transformed, but never created or destroyed within the system. Every star, every ray of light, every process in nature is not producing new energy—it is using what already exists. The universe is not generating power; it is continually transforming what was there from the beginning.

That realization changes how we see everything. If all energy within the universe has always remained constant, then it could not have originated from within the universe itself. It had to come from beyond it—brought into existence in a single, complete act.

This chapter also shows how that energy behaves. At the smallest scales, photons are produced through precise interactions, as electrons release energy and return to stability. From the light of a bulb to the power of the sun, the same underlying process connects the smallest and the largest expressions of creation. What appears ordinary is sustained by a consistent and ordered system.

But the deeper implication is not scientific—it is personal. The energy that sustains the universe is the same energy that sustains you. Every breath, every thought, every moment of life depends on what was spoken into existence at the beginning.

In the end, this chapter reveals something profound: the laws of physics do not diminish God's power—they point to it. If energy cannot create itself, yet exists in immeasurable abundance, then the One who brought it into being is not merely powerful.

He is without limit.

9 — Quantum Force and Motion

"All matter originates and exists only by virtue of a force which brings the particle of an atom to vibration and holds this most minute solar system of the atom together.

We must assume behind this force the existence of a conscious and intelligent mind. This mind is the matrix of all matter."

Max Planck
Nobel Prize in Physics (1918)
The Nature of Matter (1944)
Florence, Italy

Chapter 8 left us with a foundational truth: **energy cannot be created or destroyed.** All the energy that exists in our universe today has been here since the very beginning. It is simply stored in different forms—never added, never removed.

That truth immediately raises a practical question:

If no new energy is ever being added, where does the "power" come from—the power that moves cars, lights our homes, makes rivers flow, and keeps stars shining?

The answer is not that fresh energy arrives from somewhere outside the universe. The power we see every day is simply the result of that **original energy changing from one form into another.** A battery releases stored chemical energy as electrical energy. A falling rock converts gravitational potential energy into motion. The sun converts nuclear energy into light and heat.

At the deepest level, these transformations begin in the quantum realm—through force, fields, and motion. This chapter explores how the energy that has existed from the beginning actively produces the motion and effects we observe all around us, all while perfectly obeying the orderly laws the Creator established at the beginning.

So what exactly is this energy doing at its most fundamental level?

Energy is not an abstract idea in a textbook.

It can warm your face—or burn your skin. It can flow from the sun and light your home. It can power your car and carry you down the highway. It passes through nerves and causes your heart to beat.

Energy is not passive. It acts. It moves. It changes things.

And if energy cannot be created or destroyed, then the question is not whether it exists—but *how it moves,* and why its motion forms the *patterns* we see throughout creation.

One of those patterns appears so often it is difficult to ignore.

It leaves behind a familiar signature—the spiral.

Why are Spirals Everywhere?

Spirals seem to pop up everywhere in nature. From the gentle curve of a nautilus shell to the majestic arms of the Milky Way, the spiral is more than just a pretty pattern, it's a profound signature of the forces shaping our universe.

In this chapter we take a closer look at the connection between quantum energy and the spiral, revealing how this elegant shape reflects the deeper rhythms of existence.

At the heart of these patterns lies the **Fibonacci sequence**, a deceptively simple series of numbers where each is the sum of the two before it: 0, 1, 1, 2, 3, 5, 8, 13... and so on.[36] What's fascinating about the Fibonacci sequence is that it isn't just a random list of numbers; it appears in nature all around us. For instance, consider the swirling arms of a spiral galaxy, such as the Milky Way. The way those arms spread outward follows the Fibonacci pattern.

---

[36] Simmons, John R. Univ. of Georgia. *Fibonacci Numbers and Nature.* 4/21/2014. https://jwilson.coe.uga.edu/EMAT6680/Simmons/Essay1/6690ProjectFibonacciF.htm

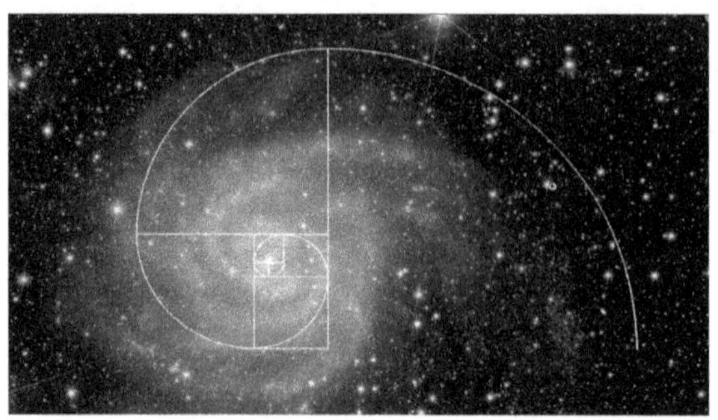

This sequence is more than a mathematical curiosity; it's a guidepost for the structures of life. As the sequence unfolds, it leads us to the **golden ratio**, a special number—approximately 1.618—that underpins beauty, balance, and growth in the natural world.

The golden ratio is everywhere.[37] It shapes the curves of galaxies, the arrangement of sunflower seeds, and even the human body. You'll find it in the proportions of famous buildings like the Parthenon, in art, and even in the growth patterns of plants. Michelangelo may have used the golden ratio when creating the Sistine Chapel and other works of art.[38] It's as if nature has a built-in blueprint, crafting elegance and efficiency from the tiniest cells to the vastness of the cosmos.

Galaxies

When you look at the stars above, you may notice

---

[37] Obermiller, Jacob. *An introduction to the golden ratio.* 12/4/2024. https://www.adobe.com/creativecloud/design/discover/golden-ratio.html

[38] Meisner, Gary. GoldenNumber.net. *Michelangelo and the Art of the Golden Ratio in Design and Composition.* 1/18/2016. https://www.goldennumber.net/michelangelo-sistine-chapel-golden-ratio-art-design/

something curious: many galaxies, especially in large clusters, form beautiful disk-like spiral shapes. These grand, distant structures are shaped by two familiar forces working together—gravity, that faithful friend that holds everything together, and something a bit more elusive called *escape velocity.*[39]

Gravity is easy enough to grasp. It keeps your feet on the ground and the planets in their orbits. Escape velocity is the minimum speed an object must reach to break free from another body's gravitational pull.

Consider the Earth: to remain in orbit around the Sun, our planet must travel at a blistering 67,000 miles per hour. Any slower and we would be pulled helplessly into the Sun. Any faster and we would be flung out into the cold darkness of space like a stone from a slingshot.

But here's the key point—escape velocity doesn't send things flying off in a straight line. Instead, objects follow graceful, curved orbits, like a runner looping around a track. The rings of Saturn provide a stunning example. The countless particles in those rings neither crash into the

[39] Ryden, Professor Barbara. Ohio State University Astronomy Department. 2/19/2003. Rotation of Our Galaxy. http://www.astronomy.ohio-state.edu/~ryden/ast162_7/notes30.html

planet nor drift away. They maintain *just the right balance of speed and gravitational pull,* creating the mesmerizing flat disk we admire from afar.

So whether we're looking at Saturn's rings or the majestic rotation of entire galaxies, it is this delicate interplay—gravity pulling inward and orbital motion pushing outward—that produces the disk-like spiral shapes we see throughout the universe.

But how do we know these galaxies are actually spinning? Picture yourself walking down the street when a police siren approaches. As it comes toward you the pitch rises; as it passes and moves away, the pitch drops. That familiar change is the Doppler Effect, first described by Christian Doppler in 1842.

The same principle applies to light. In a spinning galaxy, light from the side moving toward us shifts to a slightly higher frequency, while light from the side moving away shifts lower. This allows astronomers to measure both the fact that galaxies rotate and how fast they are turning.

And here's the remarkable discovery: galaxies aren't just spinning in place—they are also zooming away from us at astonishing speeds, each trailing magnificent spiral arms like a giant cosmic whirlpool. The largest structures in the universe are swept up in this grand, spiraling motion.

Why Spirals?

But why spirals? Why this particular shape again and again? The answer, I believe, is deeply connected to the most fundamental building block of creation itself—quantum energy.

The force of quantum energy, present from the dawn of existence, drives the movements we see on every scale, from the swirling of galaxies to the particles that form matter. It is as though the universe, in all its vastness, carries the fingerprint of its Creator in every spiraling motion we observe.

Our Solar System

What, then, does our own solar system truly look like? Most of us imagine a tidy, static diagram with the Sun at the center and planets tracing perfect circles around it. But that picture is far from reality.[40]

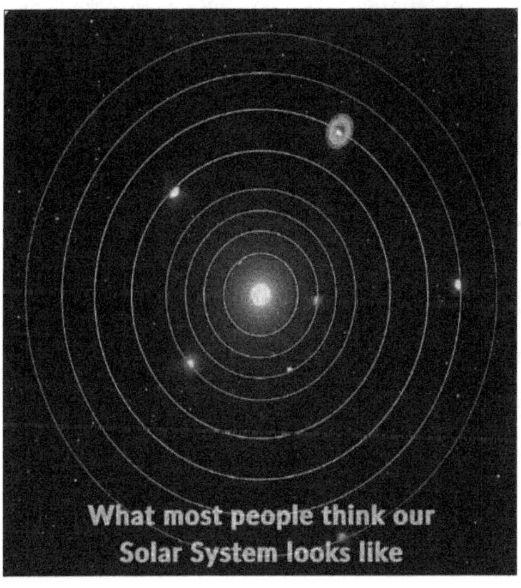

In truth, the Sun itself—along with every star in the Milky Way—is racing around the center of the galaxy at

[40] World of Engineering. @engineers_feed. (Oct. 25, 2023) https://x.com/engineers_feed/status/1717175113551122587?s=20

nearly 514,000 miles per hour, taking about 230 million years to complete one orbit.[41] As the Sun races along, the planets revolve around it in paths that are not simple circles but graceful spirals. Nothing in this universe truly stands still. Everything moves.[42]

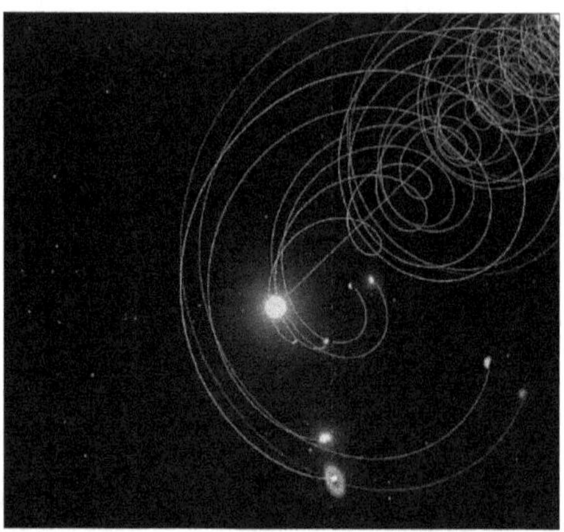

This same spiraling motion appears not only in the heavens but right here on Earth.

Hurricanes and Tornadoes

Galaxies and solar systems move in majestic spirals. Turn your attention to the Earth beneath our feet, and you see the same pattern. A hurricane, one of nature's most powerful forces, spins in a spiral—counter-clockwise in the Northern Hemisphere and clockwise in the Southern. The same is true of tornadoes.

---

[41] Waller, William H. *The Milky Way: An Insider's Guide*. Princeton University Press; First Edition (April 21, 2013)

[42] Ibid.

Have you ever wondered why? It's because of the Coriolis effect—Earth's rotation itself shapes the direction of the spiral.

DNA and Plant Life

Now narrow your gaze to something far smaller but no less wondrous: the very building blocks of life. The average adult male has 30 to 40 trillion cells, each faithfully replicating its DNA during mitosis. And what is the shape of DNA itself—the essence of our being? A spiral. More precisely, a beautiful double helix.

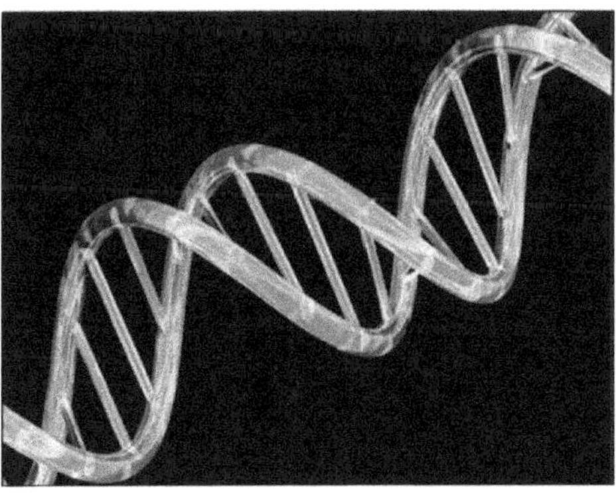

Why a spiral? It could have been a straight line, a chaotic tangle, or some strange lattice. Yet it is a spiral, formed by the same fundamental forces that shape the stars. The quantum forces that carve galaxies into spiraled beauty are quietly at work in your own cells.

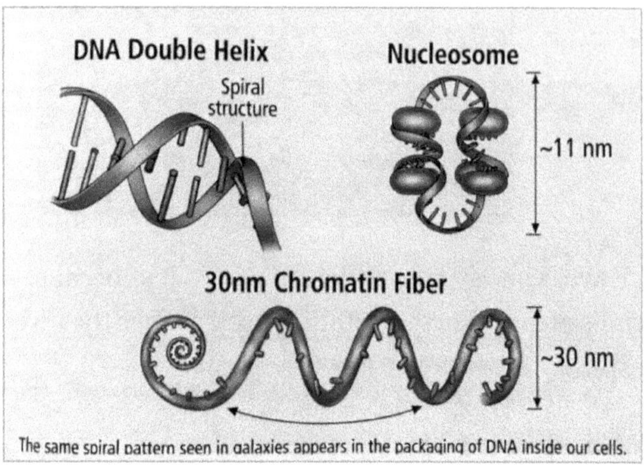

The same spiral pattern seen in galaxies appears in the packaging of DNA inside our cells.

Here, once more, we encounter that familiar form—a spiral. This time, it is found in chromatin, the substance essential for cell division. As cells prepare to split, the chromatin carefully packages the DNA, ensuring that life's blueprint is faithfully passed on. And what shape does this critical structure take? Yes, again, a spiral.

These quantum forces are not limited to planets and DNA. They appear in the quiet growth of plant life as well.[43] Certain photosynthetic bacteria, such as Rhodobacter sphaeroides, play a vital role in producing the oxygen we breathe and turning sunlight into the sugars that sustain life. And what shape do these remarkable bacteria take? Once again—a spiral.

---

43 Dr. James Allen & Professor Neal Woodbury. Arizona State University. Rhodobacter Sphaeroids. http://www.public.asu.edu/~laserweb/woodbury/research.htm

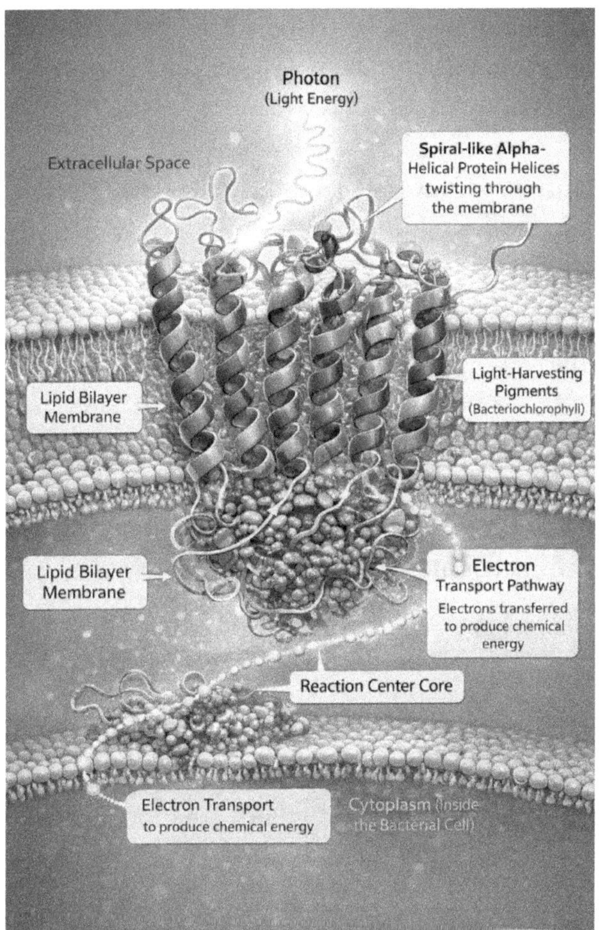

A Deeper Question

At every level of existence—from the swirling galaxies overhead to the microscopic strands within us—the spiral emerges. Is this repeated pattern simply coincidence after coincidence? Or is there a deeper explanation?

The answer lies in the unseen realm, far beneath what we can perceive with the naked eye. In the strange, subtle world of quantum energy—God's first creation—quantum fields interact in ways that give rise to the forces shaping the universe.

Quantum energy acts as an invisible architect, guiding atoms and molecules into the most efficient and stable structures. The spiral, it seems, is not arbitrary. It is the natural outcome of these forces seeking balance and harmony.

In essence, the spiral serves as nature's signature. It reflects the quantum energies at work all around us. Whether we gaze at the stars or examine the intricate design of life, we encounter the same pattern—a spiral endlessly unfolding, propelled by the mysterious and ever-present forces that connect all things.

The spiral, found from the stars above to the cells within us and the plants we eat, points to a universal truth: a common thread woven through all creation. It is not mere chance, but the signature of a greater design.

The forces that shape the galaxies are the same forces that shape the smallest elements of life. This spiral structure is evidence of a force that transcends the physical—a force present in the first moment of creation, what we now call quantum energy.

And if we trace that force back to its source, we reach a truth that cannot be ignored: it is the imprint of God's hand, present from the beginning of time, shaping everything that exists, great and small. What we see in the spiral is not merely a pattern. It is the fingerprint of the Creator—a beautiful testament to the unity of His design.

The Motion of Quantum Energy

At the quantum level, particles do not follow the same straightforward rules we see in everyday life. Energy here is constantly in motion, and particles behave in ways that often defy our ordinary understanding of motion and shape.

So what exactly is motion at this scale, and how do we describe it? To understand it better, we first need to explore a simple but powerful idea: the *vector*.

Picture, if you will, a bullet fired from a rifle. It has two distinct kinds of motion at once. First, it travels forward in a straight line—that's its linear velocity. Second, it spins rapidly around its own axis because of the rifling inside the barrel. That spin, or circular velocity, stabilizes the bullet's flight, much like the spiral motion of a football thrown by a skilled quarterback.

These two motions can be represented as two different **vectors**. One is the *linear vector*, pointing straight ahead along the bullet's path. The other is the **rotational** or **angular vector**, describing the spinning motion around its center.

Quantum energy works in a similar way. Take a photon of light, for example. It moves forward at an incredible speed while also spinning. Its **linear vector** carries it straight ahead, while its rotational vector—the photon's "spin"—adds another rich layer of motion.

Einstein showed us that nothing with mass can reach or exceed the speed of light. Photons, being massless, travel at that constant speed in a straight line—this is their linear vector. That rule holds true across the entire electromagnetic spectrum, whether we're talking about slow, gentle radio waves, the warmth of microwaves, or the visible light we see with our eyes.

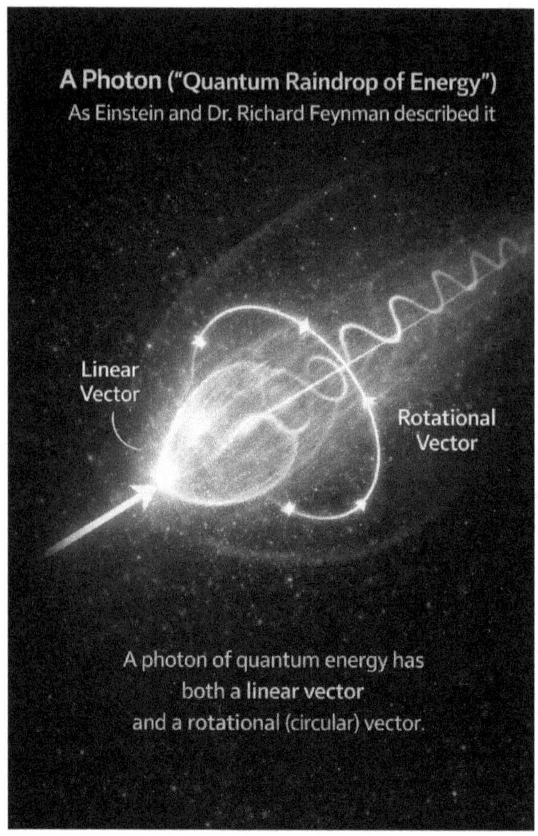

But the real intrigue begins with the photon's spinning motion. Not all light spins at the same rate. Radio waves rotate slowly, while gamma rays spin with tremendous speed. And just as a faster-spinning bullet cuts through the air more effectively, the faster a photon spins, the more energy it carries. This spinning motion is what we call **frequency**.

This is why light comes in so many different forms. The linear speed of a photon never changes, but its frequency (how fast it spins) can vary widely. Slow-spinning radio waves are gentle and low-energy. Fast-spinning gamma rays are powerful and intense. The entire spectrum of electromagnetic radiation—from radio waves to X-rays to visible light—emerges from this beautiful balance between constant forward speed and varying rotational speed.

To help picture the rotational part, imagine standing on a playground merry-go-round. As it spins faster, you feel a constant pull outward. Yet the direction of that pull is always changing—north, then east, then south—even though you're moving in a circle. A photon's rotational vector behaves much the same way: it is constantly shifting direction while staying bound to its circular motion.

The faster the merry-go-round spins, the stronger the force you feel. In the same way, the faster a photon spins (the higher its frequency), the more energy it possesses. The distance between each "spin"—what we call the **wavelength**—gets shorter as the spin quickens.

This relationship is captured in one of the most elegant equations in physics:

$$\mathbf{c = \nu \times \lambda}$$

where c is the speed of light, ν (nu) is the frequency, and λ (lambda) is the wavelength. The speed of light remains constant, but as the wavelength stretches, the frequency must slow down. When the wavelength shortens, the frequency increases. It's like a perfectly balanced see-saw—one side can only rise when the other falls.

This inverse relationship is not some mathematical trick. It is a profound truth woven into the fabric of creation. It governs every form of electromagnetic wave and explains the rich diversity of light we experience—from the slow hum of radio waves to the high-energy crackle of gamma rays.

When we study the rotational vector of a photon, we begin to see a grander picture: a universe in which light, in all its forms, obeys the same intricate and consistent laws. Whether traveling in the longest, laziest wavelengths or the shortest, most intense bursts of energy, every photon follows this elegant relationship—a law established by the Creator, as sure and unchanging as the rising of the sun or the steady motion of the stars.

Visualizing Particle Motion

The world of quantum energy can sometimes feel very abstract—tiny particles moving in ways that seem strange and invisible to our everyday experience. Thankfully, scientists have clever tools that help us make the unseen visible. One of the most beautiful is the bubble chamber.

Consider the accompanying image from Fermilab, showing the spiraling paths of particles captured in a bubble chamber.[44] These delicate, glowing lines are created when charged particles race through liquid hydrogen and ionize the atoms along their path. For a brief moment, the

---

[44] Fermilab. https://history.fnal.gov/historical/experiments/neutrino_picture.html

chamber's piston lowers the pressure, causing tiny bubbles to form exactly along those ionized trails. The result is a stunning visual record of the particles' journeys.

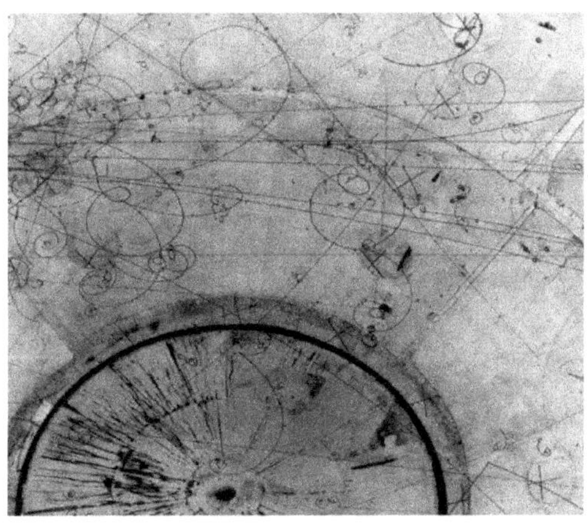

Fermilab: Neutrino Ionized Trails

The curvature and shape of these tracks tell scientists a great deal—the type of particle, its energy, its charge, and even its mass. A tighter curve often indicates a heavier or slower-moving particle, while graceful spirals stretching outward suggest lighter, faster ones. Once again, right at the smallest scales we can observe, the spiral appears.

Just as a photon carries both a linear vector (its forward motion) and a rotational vector (its spin), the intricate dance of particles in the bubble chamber reflects the same interplay of forces and energies at the quantum level. As you look at the image, each curving line tells its own story—a fleeting snapshot of the ceaseless activity that forms the hidden foundation of everything we see in the universe.

The Spring Analogy – Quantum "Raindrop"

The quantum world can feel very abstract until we find a simple way to picture it. One helpful analogy is a common spring—the kind you find inside an ordinary ballpoint pen.

Hold the spring and look at it straight on, from the end. It appears as a nearly perfect circle. Now turn it sideways. Suddenly it looks like a smooth, undulating wave—what scientists call a sine wave.

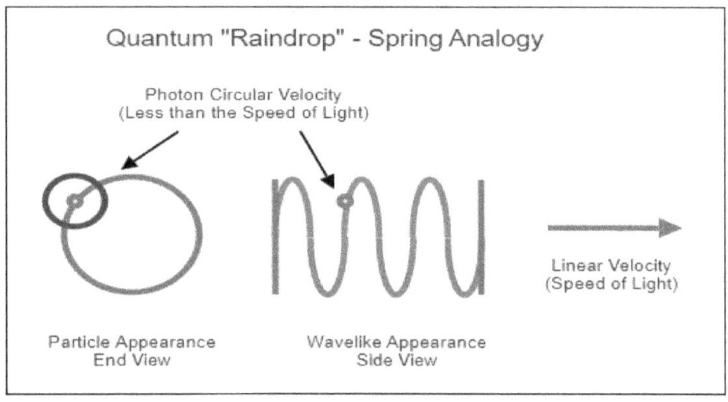

Quantum Raindrop – Spring Analogy

Now let's replace the spring with a photon of light. Imagine we have a device that can only detect the photon when it is at the very top of one of those peaks (shown as the red dot in the eBook, gray in print). As the photon travels forward, the dot would appear, disappear, and reappear. It would seem as though we are watching a strange little particle popping in and out of existence.

If instead we could view the same photon from the side, it would look like a continuous sine wave—the familiar pattern you see on an oscilloscope.

The same photon, the same motion—yet depending on how we observe it, it appears completely different. Look at it one way and it behaves like a particle. Look at it another way and it behaves like a wave. This is the famous **wave-particle duality** at the heart of quantum mechanics.

And this duality is directly tied to the properties we've been exploring: frequency, wavelength, rotation, and energy. The deeper we go, the clearer it becomes that these "strange" behaviors are not chaotic. They are part of an orderly system.

But what does this mean for the physical world we can see and touch? How do these tiny quantum motions influence everything from galaxies to DNA? That's where things get even more fascinating.

Connecting the Concepts

If quantum energy is the foundation of all matter and carries both forward motion and rotational motion, then its effects should appear at every scale—from the invisible photon to the grand spirals of galaxies and the double helix of DNA.

One of the most compelling illustrations of this connection is the idea known as the Butterfly Effect.

The Butterfly Effect

Picture the delicate flutter of a butterfly's wings—an almost imperceptible movement that, in theory, could set off a chain of atmospheric events culminating in a storm half a world away. This principle captures how small actions can, through cascading interactions, yield enormous consequences.[45]

Think of a billiard table: a single, well-placed strike sends the cue ball gliding, colliding, and redirecting the entire game. The same kind of cascading interactions play out across the cosmos. Every atom and every particle is in ceaseless motion, colliding and influencing others, sending ripples through the universe.

In the quantum realm, even the tiniest particles of light—photons—are never still. They weave together the fabric of reality, carrying energy so immense that it can be harnessed to light a city or, as in nuclear reactors, unleash power from matter scarcely larger than a pebble.

Yet amid all this activity, we do not find pure randomness. Patterns emerge. Order appears. The same quantum energy that gently warms your skin in sunlight can also power a nuclear reaction. Life-giving or devastating, its effects depend not only on tiny initial motions but on how that energy is channeled according to the consistent laws and boundaries the Creator established.

Every photon, every subatomic interaction participates in a grand equilibrium. Within this intricate dance of energy—guided by precise relationships of frequency, rotation, momentum, and force—we catch a glimpse of the

---

[45] Dizikes, Peter. "When the Butterfly Effect Took Flight". MIT Technology Review. (Feb. 22, 2011). https://www.technologyreview.com/2011/02/22/196987/when-the-butterfly-effect-took-flight/

Creator's wisdom. He set in motion forces vast enough to shape galaxies, yet precise and bounded enough to spark a single heartbeat and sustain the ordered universe we inhabit.

Rutherford and Orbiting Electrons

The journey toward understanding how quantum energy interacts with matter began with a deceptively simple experiment over a century ago. In 1911, Ernest Rutherford's groundbreaking work became the first step toward uncovering the hidden order of the universe—a design shaped by forces far smaller than the eye can see, yet powerful enough to influence the spirals of galaxies.

At the time, scientists subscribed to the **Plum Pudding Model**, imagining atoms as formless blobs with particles scattered randomly, like fruit suspended in a cake. Rutherford challenged this view with his now-famous **gold foil experiment**.[46] He fired alpha particles at a thin sheet of gold, expecting them all to pass straight through. Most did—but to his astonishment, some deflected sharply, as if they had collided with something solid and dense.

---

[46] MIT OpenCourseWare. "5.111 Principles of Chemical Science." (Fall 2008). https://ocw.mit.edu/courses/5-111-principles-of-chemical-science-fall-2008/c9a26e9bece30dc2542590b1df6fc8c1_lecnotes02.pdf

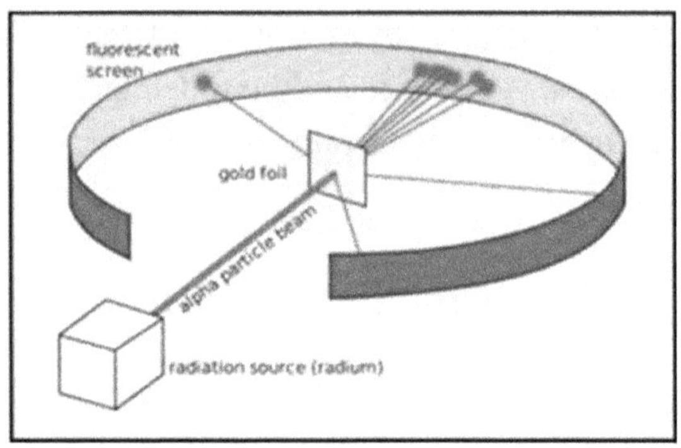

MIT: Gold Foil Experiment

This was no random arrangement. Rutherford had discovered the atom's nucleus—a compact, positively charged core orbited by electrons. The atom was not chaotic at all; it was structured, ordered, and precise.

Think of a garage door's safety sensors: a beam of infrared light stretches between them, invisible yet instantly interrupted if something crosses its path. In much the same way, Rutherford's alpha particles were "interrupted" by the nucleus of a gold atom, revealing its presence just as an object reveals itself by breaking that invisible beam.

This discovery reshaped our understanding of matter. Atoms became known as **miniature solar systems**, with electrons orbiting the nucleus like planets around a star. This insight became the foundation for quantum mechanics, where electrons occupy specific energy levels—or "shells"—and jump between them by absorbing or releasing energy.

From electrons leaping between shells to galaxies sweeping in spiral arms, the same elegant patterns emerge. The spiraling nature of quantum energy shows us a universe that is not random but exquisitely ordered—set in motion at the moment of creation. In the next chapter, my Theory of Universal Motion explores how these quantum forces are woven into the very fabric of existence.

The Quantum Leap

At the heart of every living thing, every element, and every planet lies the atom—so small it is invisible to the naked eye, yet it forms the basic building block of the entire physical universe. Understanding how atoms remain stable was one of the great turning points in modern science.

Imagine a satellite orbiting the Earth. Gravity pulls it inward, but its forward motion keeps it from falling. If it loses enough energy, it spirals inward and eventually burns up in the atmosphere. Classical physics suggested electrons should behave the same way—spiraling into the nucleus until the atom collapsed. But atoms don't collapse. Something deeper is at work.

The first major breakthrough came in 1900 from Max Planck. He was trying to solve a puzzling problem: why didn't hot objects radiate infinite amounts of energy at high frequencies, as classical theories predicted? (If they did, even an ordinary flashlight could behave like a deadly science-fiction weapon.) Planck proposed a radical idea—energy is not continuous but comes in tiny, discrete packets he called **quanta**. With his famous constant ($h = 6.6 \times 10^{-34}$ joule seconds), he showed that the energy of radiation is directly proportional to its frequency. This insight solved the puzzle and laid the foundation for quantum mechanics.

Building on Planck's work, Niels Bohr took the next bold step in 1913. He suggested that electrons do not orbit the nucleus randomly or in decaying spirals. Instead, they occupy specific, fixed energy levels—like cars restricted to certain lanes on a racetrack. Electrons can only exist in these precise orbits. To jump from one level to another, they must absorb or release an exact amount of energy—a discrete "quantum" of energy.

We call this sudden shift a **quantum leap**—a change in energy and position that happens instantly, with no in-between state. Just as you cannot stand halfway between rungs on a ladder, an electron cannot hover halfway between energy levels. It must make a clean jump, emitting or absorbing a precise packet of light in the process.

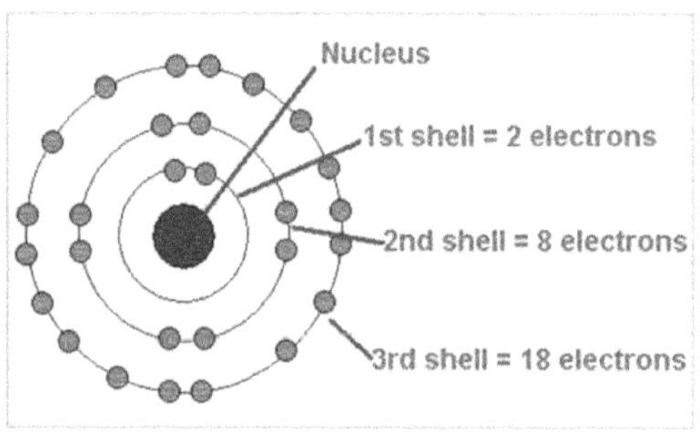

Atomic Shells

Bohr's model introduced two revolutionary ideas:

- Electrons possess quantized angular momentum — only certain discrete amounts are allowed.
- Each orbit corresponds to a specific energy level.

Using Planck's constant, Bohr calculated the energy levels for hydrogen and found they followed precise, evenly spaced steps—like rungs on a ladder. Electrons could jump from rung to rung, but never exist in between. This explained why atoms are stable: the electrons are locked into these quantized orbits and cannot spiral inward as classical physics had predicted.

Once again we encounter the quiet power of boundaries. Just as the constant speed of light sets an unbreakable limit across the universe, these quantized orbits create stable "rungs" within the atom. Our entire cosmos operates like a vast snow globe—a closed system in which energy is beautifully conserved and governed, never added, never lost, yet free to transform within the boundaries the Creator established.

Bohr's discovery revealed something profound. At the smallest scales, nature does not behave in smooth, continuous flows the way our everyday experience suggests. Instead, energy moves in orderly, discrete steps. What once looked like randomness gave way to precise, quantized beauty.

And here is one of the most beautiful insights of all: Bohr's model of the atom mirrors the cosmos itself. Electrons orbit the nucleus much like planets orbit the Sun. The same kinds of ordered laws govern both the tiniest structures and the largest.

Once again, we see the universe speaking with one consistent voice—a voice that points back to a single, intelligent Creator who established the same elegant order at every scale, from the atom to the spiraling galaxies.

Quantum Force and Motion

We began this chapter by asking why spirals appear everywhere.

Whether we look at galaxies sweeping through space, hurricanes crossing oceans, the double helix within our cells, or the ionized trails left in a bubble chamber, the same motion emerges again and again.

The spiral is not ornamentation.
It is what motion looks like when governed by law.

As we moved deeper, we found that beneath every spiral lies energy—and beneath energy, motion—and beneath motion, relationship.

A photon travels forward at 186,000 miles per second. Not faster. Not slower. That speed is not a suggestion. It is a boundary.

Within our universe, light sets a limit. Nothing with mass crosses it. Time bends as it is approached. Space itself responds to it. It is a line drawn into the structure of reality.

And within that boundary, the photon carries another constraint: frequency and wavelength are bound together by an unbreakable relationship.

If the wavelength stretches, the frequency must fall. If the frequency rises, the wavelength must shrink.

$$c = \nu \times \lambda$$

The equation doesn't express an opinion. It describes.

In that single equation, we see something extraordinary: creation speaks the language of mathematics. Relationships are not arbitrary. They are precise. They are consistent. They are discoverable.

In the same way, the photon's behavior is not chaotic motion. It is structured motion.

And yet, we do not see it directly. The photon moves too quickly. It exists on scales too small. We observe its effects. We measure interference patterns. We trace spirals in liquid hydrogen. We infer its properties through disciplined, indirect observation.

Our tools extrapolate. Our models approximate—but the order remains undeniable.

The "quantum raindrop" illustrates the mystery. Viewed one way, the photon appears circular. Viewed another, it appears as a wave. The same reality, when it is revealed differently depending on perspective. Particle and wave. Forward motion and rotation. Linear vector and rotational vector.

And from this bounded, quantized, mathematically describable motion comes everything.

The warmth on your face.

The electricity in your home.
The stability of atoms.
The oxygen in your lungs.
The rhythm of your heartbeat.

Energy does not flow in vague continuums. It moves in discrete packets. Electrons do not drift aimlessly; they occupy defined energy levels. They leap — but only in precise steps.

Quantization is not randomness—it is restriction.

And restriction is what allows stability.

The boundary that limits light stabilizes spacetime, the mathematical relationships that govern photons stabilize atoms, and the same interplay of forward motion and rotation that shapes a photon also shapes galaxies.

The smallest scale mirrors the largest.

Nothing in this universe moves without law. Nothing exceeds the boundaries inscribed into creation. The spirals we observe are not accidents; they are the visible result of energy operating within limits.

Boundaries are not weakness—they reflect design.

A universe without limits would dissolve into chaos. A universe without mathematical coherence would be unintelligible. A universe without quantization would collapse.

Instead, we find constraint. We find relationship. We find structure.

And within that structure, we find beauty.

From the speed of light to quantum leaps, from atomic structure to galactic spirals, creation reveals itself as ordered motion within defined limits.

We may not fully grasp every detail of the photon's journey. We may never observe it directly as it travels across the fabric of space. But the patterns it leaves behind testify to something deeper.

Behind the motion.
Behind the mathematics.
Behind the boundaries.

There is unity.

And unity is not an accident.

The light that moves at 186,000 miles per second does not merely illuminate the universe.

It reveals that the universe itself is governed.

Chapter 9: Summary

This chapter asks a natural next question: *if energy exists everywhere, how does it move—and why does that motion create the patterns we see throughout the universe?*

As we look more closely, a familiar pattern begins to emerge. From galaxies and solar systems to hurricanes, DNA, and even microscopic particles, the same shape appears again and again—the spiral. This pattern is not incidental. It reflects the way energy moves when governed by consistent forces at every level of creation.

At the quantum level, that motion becomes even more precise. Light moves forward at a fixed speed, yet it also carries a rotational motion that determines its energy. These relationships are not random. They are governed by exact mathematical laws that hold everything in balance—from the stability of atoms to the structure of the cosmos.

Even when quantum behavior appears mysterious—whether in interference patterns, wave-particle duality, or entanglement—it does not reflect chaos. It reflects order that we are only beginning to understand. The same principles that guide the smallest particles also shape the largest structures, linking the microscopic and the cosmic in one continuous system.

In the end, this chapter reveals that motion in the universe is not unbounded. It operates within defined limits—limits that make stability, structure, and life possible. The spirals we observe are not accidents; they are the result of energy moving according to those laws.

And those laws point to something deeper:

The universe is not only filled with energy.
It is governed.

10 — Connecting Energy and Motion

"He is before all things, and in him all things hold together."

Colossians 1:17

If creation began with God's command, and if motion unfolds within physical law, then are these patterns just coincidence, or do they follow deeper laws?

The order we observed in light—the unity between frequency, wavelength, energy, and momentum—does not just happen. It is enforced by constants. Among them stands one of the most astonishing numbers ever discovered: Planck's constant.

It is small beyond imagination, yet it governs the scale of reality.

Planck's constant does not describe light in isolation. It defines how energy itself is permitted to exist. It determines how light carries energy, how electrons occupy space, how motion becomes quantized rather than continuous. Without it, there would be no discrete energy levels, no stable atoms, no structured matter.

The previous chapter showed that motion is conserved and patterns recur. This chapter presses deeper:

What prevents energy from flowing as a smooth, unbroken continuum?

What makes it move in distinct steps instead of blending together without limits?

The answer lies not in material structure but in a fundamental boundary written into the fabric of the universe.

The Connection Between Frequency and Energy

Light carries energy in discrete packets called photons. The energy of each photon is not determined by mass (it has none) but by how rapidly it oscillates—its frequency (f). This relationship is expressed in one of the most important equations in physics:

$$\mathbf{E = h\,f}$$

Where:

- E is the energy of the photon,
- h is Planck's constant (6.626×10^{-34} J·s),
- f is the frequency.

This deceptively simple expression reveals something profound: energy is not arbitrary. It comes in measurable, proportional relationships governed by a universal scale.

The same constant that governs photons also governs electrons. The same constant that quantizes light, quantizes motion. The universe does not merely move—it moves in permitted increments.

Energy is not free to take any value. Motion is not infinitely divisible. Reality is structured at its foundation.

And that structure is anchored by Planck's constant.

The Quantization of Motion

Planck's constant does more than govern photons. It also quantizes the motion of matter. Electrons orbiting an atom's nucleus cannot occupy arbitrary paths. They are restricted to specific energy levels. In the Bohr model, this is expressed through **angular momentum**:

$$\mathbf{L = n\ (h\ /\ 2\pi)}$$

Where:

- L is the angular momentum of the electron
- n is an integer (1, 2, 3, etc.), representing the electron's quantum number
- h is Planck's constant
- $h/2\pi$ is the angular momentum

The electron can only stand on certain "steps" of a staircase whose spacing is set by h. This quantization prevents electrons from spiraling into the nucleus and makes stable atoms—and therefore chemistry and life—possible. Motion itself is not infinitely divisible. It comes in structured increments.

From Light to Kinetic Energy

When photons interact with matter, they demonstrate how light energy becomes motion. In the photoelectric effect, a photon strikes a material and ejects an electron if its frequency is high enough. The kinetic energy of the ejected electron is given by:

$$E_{kinetic} = h f - \phi$$

where ϕ is the minimum energy (work function) needed to free the electron.

Here the bridge between the quantum and the everyday becomes visible. A photon—massless, intangible—transfers its quantized energy and sets an electron in motion. The same principle that governs light also produces tangible kinetic energy in the material world.

This connection appears even in ordinary experience. A fast-rolling bowling ball carries far more kinetic energy than a slow one. Scale that idea down dramatically: a high-frequency photon delivers a sharper "kick" to an electron than a low-frequency one. Light, though without mass, can drive motion because its energy is real and precisely portioned.

A Unified Picture: Frequency, Energy, and Motion

The relationship between frequency, energy, and motion forms the backbone of the dynamics of the universe. This unity reflects God's intricate design, governing everything from subatomic particles to celestial bodies. Such harmony reveals the Creator's hand in every aspect of all that exists.

Planck's constant ties together seemingly separate phenomena into a single, unified picture:

- **Frequency** determines energy, whether in light waves or electrons.
- **Energy levels** within atoms are quantized, creating order out of potential chaos.
- **Kinetic energy** can arise when light interacts with matter, transferring energy to create motion.

The same constant that governs a photon also governs the stability of electrons and atoms. The universe does not run on separate rulebooks. It speaks one consistent language—from the smallest quantum interaction to the motion of macroscopic objects.

Sustained Within Boundaries

Planck's constant is not decorative. It is a limit. A scale. A boundary.

Without it, energy would blur into a continuous smear with no structure. Atoms would collapse. Matter would dissolve. Instead, energy arrives in defined packets, electrons occupy defined levels, and motion proceeds in permitted increments.

The universe is full of such boundaries: the speed of light, the curvature of spacetime, conserved quantities that cannot be violated. These are not arbitrary restrictions. They are the conditions that make stability, chemistry, stars, and life possible.

Growth without boundary collapses. Freedom without structure becomes chaos. In creation, limits are not the enemies of possibility—they are its guardians.

Colossians declares, “In Him all things hold together.” Physics does not replace this truth. It shows how the holding together occurs. Constants define the scale. Conservation ensures persistence. Boundaries provide stability.

Energy does not dissolve.

Motion does not fragment.

Structure does not collapse.

It holds together—because it is bounded.

Chapter 10: Summary

This chapter began with a question: *Are the patterns of energy and motion coincidence, or do they rest on deeper law?*

The evidence is clear. Energy does not flow arbitrarily. Motion is not free to take any form. Both operate within precise limits set by constants—most notably Planck’s constant.

What we observe in light is the same order that stabilizes atoms and allows kinetic energy to emerge when light meets matter. The universe is not a collection of disconnected systems but a single coherent whole.

Most importantly, these boundaries are not limitations on God's power. They are expressions of it. They prevent chaos and sustain the ordered cosmos we inhabit. Within these God-established limits, everything holds together—moment by moment—just as Scripture declares.

11 — Energy, Motion, and Design

"But all things become visible when they are exposed by the light, for everything that becomes visible is light."

Eph. 5:13 (NASB)

In the previous chapter, we saw that the universe is governed by limits. Constants such as Planck's constant and the speed of light establish boundaries that cannot be crossed. These limits are not constraints—they are structures of stability.

But do these constants and laws point to a deeper organizing principle?

Boundaries by themselves do not cause anything to move. A speed limit does not make a car drive. The walls of a stadium do not make the players run.

Now we must ask: What moves upon that cosmic stage? What forces operate within those divine limits?

The answer lies in magnetism, angular momentum, and

the hidden architecture of energy itself.

Magnetic Moments

The relationship between light and matter reveals a profound interplay at the heart of physics. Just as light influences motion, magnetic fields exert torque on matter. Earth's magnetic field, for example, directs the needle of a compass—not by contact, but by an invisible force that has existed from the moment of creation.

Light and magnetism may appear separate, yet they are deeply intertwined within the fabric of creation. Scripture describes light as a cloak stretched across the heavens (Psalm 104:2), an image that resonates with what physics has uncovered: fields permeate space, governing how energy behaves from the smallest particle to the largest structure, from common occurrences to the extreme conditions near black holes.

Physicist Richard Feynman helped clarify how particles possess a measurable property known as a *magnetic moment*.[47] This property determines how particles, atoms, and molecules respond to magnetic fields. When a compass aligns northward, it is responding to Earth's magnetic moment—an unseen torque acting with precision and consistency.

The same principle operates in medical imaging. In an MRI, protons align with a powerful magnetic field. A burst of radiofrequency energy disrupts that alignment, and as the

---

47 Richard P. Feynman, QED, the strange theory of light and matter. 2006 by Princeton University Press. 117.

protons return to equilibrium, they emit signals that form detailed images of the human body.

These interactions scale upward. Electromagnetic fields influence matter in environments as vast as galaxies and as extreme as black holes. The connection between the microscopic and the cosmic is not symbolic—it is structural. The same invisible forces operate at every level.

Magnetic moments are not abstract curiosities. They are measurable expressions of how energy interacts with fields. And wherever magnetic moments exist, force is present.

Amplifying Photon Frequency and Energy

At the heart of exploration of magnetic fields lies the Zeeman Effect, a discovery by physicist Pieter Zeeman in 1896. This phenomenon reveals how magnetic fields alter the frequency and energy of photons.

Imagine a spinning bullet encountering a magnetic field. If its spin aligns with the field, the field captures it; otherwise, it passes through, its energy subtly transformed. A similar principle applies to photons, whose frequencies shift when influenced by magnetic fields.

The Zeeman Effect reveals a stunning truth; magnetic fields can alter the frequency of photons, changing their energy. Why is this important? This is foundational for understanding extreme environments such as black holes, where powerful electromagnetic and gravitational fields interact with light and matter, bending space and driving photons to high energy levels.

How Magnetic Moments Interact

Every entity possessing quantum energy—from photons to atoms and molecules, and even the matter composing our bodies—has a magnetic moment. In essence, all matter exhibits this property.

The magnetic moment is harnessed in practical applications such as metal detectors. These devices rely on an electromagnetic field to locate hidden metallic objects. When the field encounters metal, the object's magnetic moment modifies the field, leading to an increase in current and an audible alert.

Magnetic moments provide a tangible connection between theoretical physics and practical application.[48] Without them, technologies like MRI machines would not exist.

Magnetic mines used during wartime serve as a stark example of the practical consequences of magnetic moments. These mines generate an electromagnetic field similar to that used in detection systems. When ships or submarines approach, their magnetic signatures disrupt the field, triggering detonation.

The same forces that move the needle of a compass also move the Earth, the Sun, atoms, and molecules. Quantum energy, such as light, radio waves, and X-rays, all exhibit magnetic moments, influencing their interactions with magnetic fields.

---

[48] Griffith, James. Introduction to Electrodynamics, 4th Edition. Cambridge University Press; 4th edition (June 29, 2017).

Understanding magnetic moments is essential to understanding the structure of the universe. The forces that shape the stars are the same forces at work in the world around you.

Magnetic Moments and Force

While magnetic moments reveal how forces shape and influence matter, they are only one part of the intricate interplay between energy and motion. To fully appreciate the interconnectedness of these forces, we turn to angular momentum, a concept that governs rotation and spin from the microscopic world of photons to the vastness of galaxies.

Angular momentum is a way to describe how something is spinning or rotating. It's similar to the idea of regular momentum (how hard it is to stop something that's moving), but for things that are spinning instead of moving in a straight line. It helps us understand how things rotate, from spinning toys like tops to planets orbiting in space. For example, the Earth keeps spinning because of its angular momentum, and changes in that momentum can tell scientists a lot about what's happening inside or around the Earth.

In the late 20th century, physicists discovered that light could carry angular momentum, despite its lack of mass.[49] This "angular momentum" of light is termed "**orbital angular momentum**" (OAM). Some physicists may refer to this as *twisting* light wavefronts, but it is actually

---

[49] Padgett, Miles and Allen, Les. "Orbital Angular Momentum in Optical Waves". Copyright © 2011 Wiley-VCH Verlag GmbH & Co. KGaA.

changing, rather than twisting, the "angular velocity" of the light waves.

When a spinning raindrop of light interacts with matter, a portion of its photons can be absorbed by the object, while others may be reflected or refracted. The absorbed photons transfer their momentum to the object, thereby causing it to move or rotate. This phenomenon, known as *light-induced torque*, showcases the intricate dance between energy and motion.

On a cosmic scale, the angular momentum of light contributes to the swirling motions of stars, galaxies, and black holes. It's another layer in the interconnectedness of the universe, where microscopic phenomena mirror the grand motions of the heavens.

Energy, Motion, and Design

Magnetic moments do not choose their direction.
They align.

Photons do not resist magnetic fields.
Their frequency shifts.

Angular momentum does not improvise.
It conserves.

From the compass needle driven toward north to protons aligning inside an MRI, from metal hulls triggering magnetic mines to galaxies spiraling around invisible centers—motion responds to structure.

Energy does not wander freely through chaos.

It operates within fields.

Light bends.
Matter aligns.
Spin transfers.
Fields govern.

At every scale, from the quantum to the cosmic, motion unfolds within boundaries already established.

This is not random. It is coordinated interaction. It is power operating under rule.

The universe does not invent its own laws.

It responds to them—and response implies authority.

The same architecture that allows physicians to see inside the human body governs the collapse of stars into black holes.

Order at every scale.
Power within limits.
Motion operating under rules.

Energy moves.

But it does not rule.

Chapter 11: Summary

This chapter moves one step further by asking: *if the universe is governed by limits, what forces are at work within those limits?*

The answer is not found in abstract theory, but in observable interaction. Magnetic fields, angular momentum, and the behavior of light all reveal that energy does not move aimlessly. It responds. It aligns. It transfers motion through consistent and measurable forces.

From a compass pointing north to the detailed images produced by an MRI, these principles are not distant or theoretical—they are active in everyday life. The same forces that guide a magnetic needle also influence atoms, shape matter, and extend outward to the motion of stars and galaxies.

This chapter also shows that light itself participates in this structure. Through its interaction with magnetic fields and its ability to transfer momentum, even massless energy can influence motion. What appears intangible carries real force, linking the smallest interactions to the largest movements in the universe.

At every level, the pattern is consistent. Energy operates within fields. Motion follows structure. Forces interact in ways that are predictable and ordered.

In the end, this chapter reveals something essential: energy does not govern itself. It responds to laws already in place.

And that response points beyond the motion itself—to the One who established the order it follows.

12 — The Theory of Universal Motion

"You believe in the God who plays dice, and I in complete law and order in a world which objectively exists, and which I, in a wildly speculative way, am trying to capture."

Albert Einstein
September 7, 1944
Letter to Max Born

The previous chapters show that quantum energy is not chaotic. It is structured. Light is governed by measurable relationships—frequency, wavelength, energy, momentum — bound together by constants that do not waver.

But if motion at the smallest scales is governed by laws, a deeper question emerges:

Do these laws point to a deeper organizing principle?

If angular momentum is intrinsic to light (quanta)—if

spin and rotational symmetry are built into the foundation of matter—then perhaps what we observe in storms, seashells, and spiral galaxies is not coincidence. Perhaps the recurrence of rotational patterns across scales reflects a deeper continuity embedded in creation itself.

What follows is not a replacement of established physics, but an attempt to follow that continuity.

A New Proposal

God's first act of creation set energy and order in motion. From this foundation I propose the **Theory of Universal Motion**:

Definition: *Angular momentum* serves as the persistent thread connecting motion across scales. Quantum entities (photons, field excitations, and particles) carry *intrinsic spin* and, in many cases, orbital angular momentum. Together with conservation laws and field interactions, these microscopic rotational properties act as seeds for the spiral and rotational patterns we see from the quantum realm all the way to galactic structures.

This proposal does not replace established physics. It follows the evidence: the same forces that govern light and matter at the smallest scales continue to shape larger phenomena under the right conditions. It aligns beautifully with the scriptural declaration "Let there be light" (Genesis 1:3), where creation begins with energy, which not only follows physical laws, but establishes them.

What This Theory Is—and Is Not

- **It is:** A unifying idea that treats **angular momentum** as a persistent, law-governed feature shaping the motion and patterns of matter across scales.

- **Is not:** A claim that all particles literally trace spirals, that all particles move at the speed of light, or that quantum outcomes are fully predetermined in violation of quantum statistics.

Rationale

At the smallest scales, particles show wave–particle duality and carry spin—an intrinsic form of angular momentum. Some light fields can also carry orbital angular momentum through a helical phase structure, though not all do and not by default.

Photons travel at the speed of light in empty space. In materials their group velocity slows down, and massive particles never reach that speed. This theory does not claim every particle follows a predetermined spiral path. Instead, it highlights the constant presence of angular momentum and how it influences the way systems develop when forces, fields, and boundaries are present.

From the micro to the macro, we see the same principle at work. Spiral arms in galaxies, cyclones, seashells, and certain chemical patterns do not mean every particle moves in a spiral. They show how conservation of angular momentum, combined with rotation and gradients, can produce similar beautiful forms across vastly different scales. The micro-level angular momentum, always present in nature, provides the seed. Under the right conditions, it grows into the familiar structures we recognize.

Macroscopic celestial mechanics and microscopic quantum events belong to different regimes, yet both are ruled by the same conservation laws. The unity is not in identical paths, but in shared symmetries that echo from quanta to galaxies.

In short, the universe often shows a domino-like effect—a small beginning triggering results on a much larger scale, sometimes dramatically.

Tentative Predictions & Touchpoints

These ideas flow naturally from thinking about the very first moments of creation and the extreme conditions we see today, such as the event horizons of black holes. I am not claiming new discoveries here—only noticing where the presence of angular momentum might show itself more clearly.

- **Light carrying rotation:** In places with strong rotation or uneven conditions—like swirling plasmas around stars or near the violent edges of black holes—we might expect to find more light that carries its own twist (what physicists call orbital angular momentum). The polarization patterns of that light could reflect the handedness of the system itself.

- **Handedness in the universe:** From the earliest moments of creation, small left-right differences may have appeared. We might one day detect subtle biases in how radiation or matter behaves in deep space or in the leftover glow from the Big Bang—echoes of the first ordering of energy.

- **Patterns that scale up:** Wherever rotation meets boundaries or constraints, we should see spiral and swirling forms appearing in predictable ways. The same principle that seeds tiny quantum twists can, under the right conditions, grow into the majestic arms of galaxies or the spirals we see in storms.

These are not strict laboratory predictions but quiet expectations: if angular momentum truly threads through creation from the beginning, then its signature should keep showing up—from the birth of the universe to its most dramatic edges.

The Photon Coherence Framework

When I first began organizing the relationships that govern light, the idea came to me in the form of a wheel—much like the familiar Ohm's Law wheel used in electrical engineering. The Photon Coherence Framework is not a new law; it is a visual way to bring together relationships that are already well known.

Frequency, wavelength, energy, momentum, and power are usually taught separately in textbooks. Yet each equation is correct. As I worked with them, the picture matured into something clearer: a centered framework with frequency at the heart.

Unlike Ohm's Law, there is no single equation that ties everything together. Instead, we have a tightly interwoven set of relationships governed by two constants — Planck's constant h and the speed of light c. When arranged coherently, frequency stands out as the governing variable.

In the diagram on the next page, frequency sits at the center. From it flow:

- Wavelength: $\lambda = c/f$
- Energy: $E = hf$
- Momentum: $p = E/c = hf/c$
- Power: $P = N \times hf$ (where N is the number of photons per second)

This is not new physics. It is structural clarity. My original "wheel" idea tried to make the relationships visible. The Photon Coherence Framework does this more faithfully — not as a circle, but as a centered relational picture. Frequency belongs in the center because it is foundational. Once you know it, the other properties follow naturally through conserved relationships.

Light, therefore, is not governed by disconnected formulas. It is governed by an internally coherent structure. The same constants thread through every part. What at first looks fragmented resolves into elegance.

The significance is not merely mathematical. If the first command in Genesis was "Let there be light," then the first physical reality introduced into creation was not chaotic energy, but energy already structured by law.

The Photon Coherence Framework

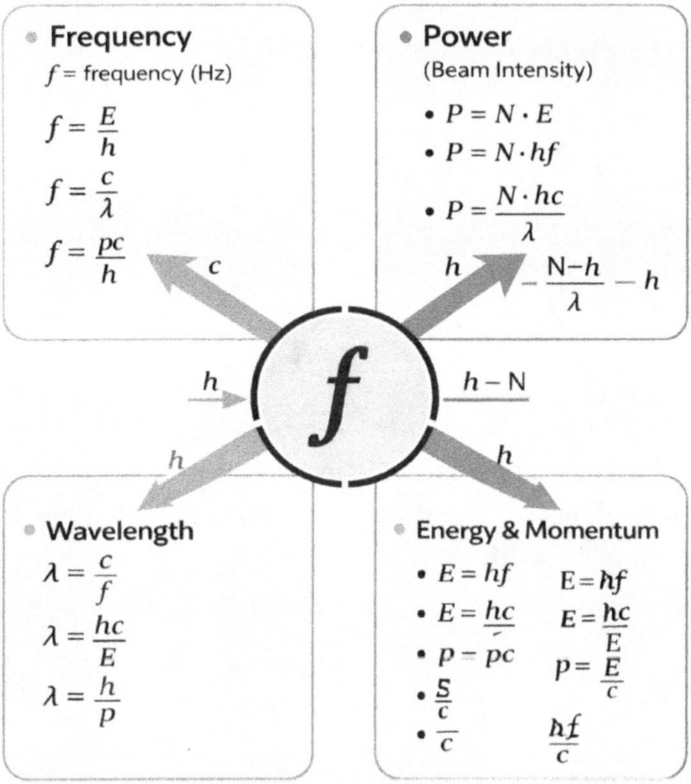

Frequency

f = frequency (Hz)

$$f = \frac{E}{h}$$

$$f = \frac{c}{\lambda}$$

$$f = \frac{pc}{h}$$

Power

(Beam Intensity)

- $P = N \cdot E$
- $P = N \cdot hf$
- $P = \frac{N \cdot hc}{\lambda}$

c h $\frac{N-h}{\lambda}$ h

h f $h - N$

h h

Wavelength

$$\lambda = \frac{c}{f}$$

$$\lambda = \frac{hc}{E}$$

$$\lambda = \frac{h}{p}$$

Energy & Momentum

- $E = hf$ $E = hf$
- $E = \frac{hc}{}$ $E = \frac{hc}{E}$
- $p = pc$ $p = \frac{E}{c}$
- $\frac{S}{c}$
- $\frac{}{c}$ $\frac{hf}{c}$

c = speed of light (2.998×10^8 m/s)

h = Planck's constant (6.626×10^{-34} Js)

N = number of photons per second

Quadrant 1: Frequency, the Governing Variable

For a photon, frequency (f) is foundational. Frequency is the number of complete wave cycles or oscillations that pass a fixed point in a specific amount of time. Measured in hertz (Hz), where 1 Hz equals one cycle per second, it defines how rapidly a wave vibrates. High-frequency waves have more energy and shorter wavelengths.

$$f = \frac{E}{h}$$

$$f = \frac{c}{\lambda}$$

$$f = \frac{pc}{h}$$

Quadrant 2. Power

Power (P) in physics is defined as the rate at which work is done, or energy is transferred or converted over time. It is measured in watts.

$$P = NE$$

$$P = Nhf$$

$$P = \frac{Nhc}{\lambda}$$

Quadrant 3. Wavelength

Wavelength is the spatial distance between two consecutive, corresponding points of the same phase in a wave, such as from crest to crest or trough to trough. It represents the length of one complete cycle of a wave, commonly denoted by the Greek letter lambda (λ) and measured in meters.

$$\lambda = \frac{c}{f}$$
$$\lambda = \frac{hc}{E}$$
$$\lambda = \frac{h}{p}$$

Quadrant 4. Energy & Momentum Without Mass

One of the most striking relationships is Momentum: Unlike classical matter, photon momentum does not arise from mass. It arises from energy itself. Directional motion and energy magnitude are directly proportional.

Photon energy is the discrete amount of energy (*E*) carried by a single photon (light particle), directly proportional to its electromagnetic frequency (*f*) and inversely proportional to its wavelength. It is calculated in joules (J).

$$E = hf$$
$$E = \frac{hc}{\lambda}$$
$$E = pc$$
$$p = \frac{E}{c} = \frac{h}{\lambda}$$

The Logic of Creation

The Photon Coherence Framework shows that light is not governed by scattered formulas but by an internally coherent structure. The Theory of Universal Motion simply extends this same insight outward.

Angular momentum – whether the intrinsic spin of quantum particles or the orbital motion of galaxies – reappears across the universe. Not as identical behavior, but as conserved symmetry. Not as forced repetition, but as lawful coherence.

Light is structured.

Motion is conserved.

Patterns recur.

When we place these truths side by side, something profound appears: the universe is not merely active–it is ordered.

Genesis 1:3 records the first creative command: "Let there be light." In physical terms, this was the emergence of energy governed by law. From that moment, every spin, every orbit, and every wave has unfolded within conserved relationships and boundaries. Creation is dynamic motion governed by design.

The spiral arms of galaxies, the rotation of storms, the handedness of molecules, and the polarization of light all arise from shared symmetries woven into creation's fabric. These laws do not merely regulate the universe – they reveal its architecture. And architecture implies intention.

This does not require pushing God into gaps of ignorance. The laws themselves are the evidence. They are stable, intelligible, and astonishingly consistent across scales separated by trillions of orders of magnitude.

The deeper we look, the more unity we find.

My proposed Theory of Universal Motion does not claim every particle traces a spiral or that every outcome is predetermined. It proposes something simpler and more profound: that the conserved order present at the smallest scales naturally cascades into recognizable structure at the largest scales. The universe is lawful at its foundation—and that lawfulness is not accidental.

If light was the first command, then order was the first gift. From photon to galaxy, motion carries the memory of its origin. And that origin was not chaos. It was a command.

Chapter 12: Summary

This chapter draws together the ideas from previous chapters and asks a deeper question: *if energy, motion, and patterns show such consistency across creation, do they point to a unifying principle?*

The answer proposed here is the Theory of Universal Motion—the idea that angular momentum, built into the smallest scales of quantum reality, continues to shape motion and patterns at every level. From the spin of particles to the rotation of galaxies, motion is connected through conserved relationships that persist across vastly different scales.

The chapter also presents the Photon Coherence Framework, a clearer way to see how frequency, wavelength, energy, momentum, and power form one unified system governed by unchanging constants.

The key insight is this: the same underlying symmetries and laws shape how systems develop. Patterns such as spirals, rotation, and alignment are not accidents. They arise because motion itself is structured at its foundation.

In the end, this chapter reveals a universe that is not only active, but ordered and unified. And that unity points beyond mere mechanism—it points to intention.

13 — Reverse Engineering Relativity

"God used beautiful mathematics in creating the universe."

Paul Dirac
Reminiscences about a Great Physicist (1990)

We have seen that the universe operates under authority — motion within limits, power within law. Boundaries do not weaken reality; they preserve it.

But what happens when motion approaches its ultimate boundary?

What happens when we push velocity to its extreme?

Classical physics had governed motion for centuries. Additive velocities worked for rivers, cannonballs, and planets. But when scientists turned their attention to light, something refused to cooperate.

The speed of light was a problem—a problem that struck at the foundation of classical physics.

No matter how fast the observer moved, no matter how fast the source traveled, the speed of light remained unchanged.

It was not a minor anomaly.

It was a fracture in the foundation.

And in wrestling with that fracture, Einstein uncovered something far deeper than a velocity problem.

He discovered that time itself was part of the equation.

Navigating Rivers and Additive Velocities

Einstein's groundbreaking work on the nature of light was motivated by a profound question: How could the speed of light remain constant, no matter the motion of the observer or the source of the light?

The principle of *additive velocities*—a concept that governed everyday experiences for centuries, suddenly became a problem for Einstein when he attempted to establish a relationship between energy and matter.

To understand the principle of additive velocities, let's examine how the Lewis and Clark Expedition used this principle to navigate the rivers of the Northwest Territory.

Lewis and Clark Understood Additive Velocities

In 1804 Meriwether Lewis and William Clark were

commissioned by President Thomas Jefferson to establish a route to the Pacific Ocean through the Northwest Territory. They traveled on rivers during most of the trip.

When they traveled downstream with a 5 mile per hour river current, they could relax and easily drift along toward their destination. If they decided to paddle at the rate of 5 mph, they would add to the speed of the river and travel at a rapid pace of 10 mph, making their journey easier and faster.

In 1806, after spending the winter near present-day Astoria, Oregon, they began their journey back east and faced the challenging task of navigating upstream against the current of the Columbia and Missouri rivers. This upstream trip was particularly arduous, as it required physical exertion and careful navigation through the rivers' currents and obstacles.

During their return trip, when the current was 5 mph upstream and they paddled 5 mph against it, they would stay at the same spot, not moving an inch. To overcome the river current, they would have to exert an incredible amount of effort to make progress.

What the Lewis and Clark Expedition experienced during their years on the rivers of the Northwest Territory was the principle of "additive velocities". They knew that the best time to travel upstream was when the rivers were low and the current was weaker. And the best time to travel downstream was usually after heavy rain when the current was strong, but not too strong. The current either added to or subtracted from their efforts, determining how fast they traveled relative to the countryside.

Interestingly, there's more to the concept of additive velocities than experienced when navigating a river; it fails to work when it comes to quantum energy.

The Additive Velocity Problem and Quantum Energy

The principle of additive velocities works seamlessly for everyday experiences, like a boat traveling on a river. However, it falls apart when we consider the speed of light. Let's return to the boat scenario and imagine that instead of paddling, you are holding a flashlight and shining its beam straight ahead, in alignment with your direction.

From your perspective in the boat, the light from the flashlight moves away from you at the speed of light, approximately 186,000 miles per second. If additive velocities applied, as they do with the boat and river current, then to a person standing on the bank, the light from your flashlight should appear to travel at the speed of the river current (5 mph) plus the speed of light.

But this is not what happens. No matter the motion of the boat, the river current, or the person observing from the bank, the speed of light remains constant at 186,000 miles per second. It doesn't matter whether the boat is moving downstream, upstream, or standing still—light always travels at the same speed relative to both you and the observer on the bank.

The fact that the speed of light remains unchanged, regardless of changes in conditions or movement, defies the principle of additive velocities and classical relativity.

Einstein's groundbreaking insight into this phenomenon revolutionized physics. He realized that time, space, and motion must be interconnected in a way that ensures the speed of light remains constant for every observer, regardless of their relative motion to the source of light or each other. This realization became the foundation of the theory of Special Relativity, which replaced the classical understanding of additive velocities and reshaped our conception of space and time.

Reverse Engineering Einstein's Special Relativity

When the "Theorem of Addition of Velocities" did not apply to the speed of light, Einstein sought to understand why. To grasp his reasoning, we will start with his equation on relativity and then work backward to reverse-engineer his logic.

Einstein's equation ($E=mc^2$) is one of the most famous equations in physics and is a fundamental principle of the theory of relativity. The equation states that the energy (E) of an object is equal to its mass (m) multiplied by the speed of light (c) squared. In mathematical terms, it can be expressed as:

$$E = mc^2$$

Here's a breakdown of what each symbol represents:

- E = Energy
- M = Mass
- C = Speed of light in a vacuum

This equation introduced a revolutionary idea: mass and

energy are not separate quantities, but different expressions of the same physical reality. Mass can be viewed as concentrated energy, and energy possesses mass-equivalent properties.

The implications are extraordinary. Because the speed of light ($c \approx 3 \times 10^8$ meters per second) is such a large number, squaring it produces an enormous multiplier. As a result, even a small amount of mass corresponds to an immense amount of energy.

This principle explains how stars produce energy, how nuclear reactions release power, and why matter itself contains stored energy even when at rest.

But how did Einstein arrive at such a conclusion?

To answer that question, we must retrace the logical steps he followed when confronted with the constancy of light.

Step 1: The Principle of Relativity

Einstein's first logical step in 1905 was deceptively simple but profoundly disruptive. He recognized that classical physics did not fail universally—it failed conditionally.[50] Its laws worked reliably, but only within a defined boundary: an **inertial frame of reference**.

In other words, Newton's laws were not wrong. *They were limited.*

---

[50] Albert Einstein. Relativity, the Special and General Theory, (New York, Crown Publishers Inc., 1961), page 44.

An inertial frame of reference is a coordinate system that is either at rest or moving at a constant velocity. Within that boundary, the familiar rules of motion – including additive velocities – operate consistently and predictably. A boat's speed can be added to the river's current.[51] Forces produce proportional accelerations. Time flows uniformly.

But that reliability exists inside a defined domain.

Einstein's insight was to recognize that the principle of additive velocities was not universally applicable – it was bounded. It worked when applied to objects moving at ordinary speeds within inertial frames, but when applied to light, it broke down.

Rather than abandon order, Einstein tightened the boundary.

He began by asking: What assumptions are truly universal, and which operate only within limits?

For example, if you were to give me a set of coordinates for New York City, I could enter the latitude and longitude, the x and y, into Google Maps and find its location relative to me. I doubt if you give much thought to the elevation of New York, the z, compared to sea level, but if you switch to "terrain view", you will see it. Regardless, Google maps show you where New York is and how to get there.

[51] Ibid.

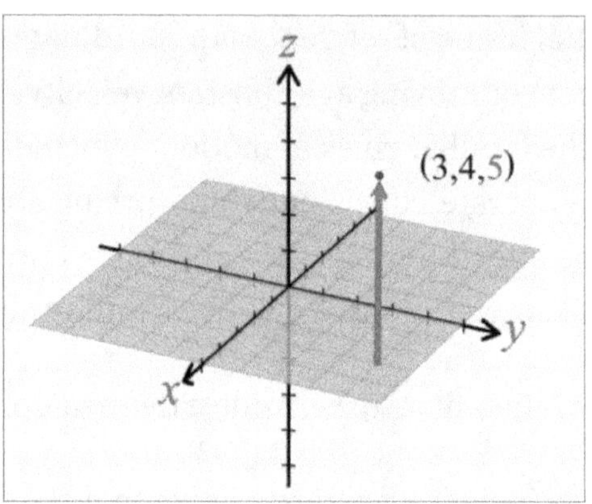

However, if you are traveling to Denver, the mile high city, and your car does not operate well at high altitudes, the coordinate "z", relative to sea level, becomes exceedingly important. While the z value of sea level is zero, the z value of Denver is 5,280 feet.

In another example, to find the location of a light bulb hanging from a ceiling, you may envision something like the figure shown above. You may measure 3 feet from one wall (the x-axis), 4 feet from another wall (the y-axis), and 5 feet up from the floor (the z-axis). You would need all these measurements to determine the location of the light bulb in 3-dimensional space. Since we don't live in 2-dimensional space but in a 3-dimensional one, every object including us has its own coordinate system. And every object within an object, like a chair inside a room, is relative to the coordinate systems of one another.

This brings us to an interesting question: what does it mean for something to be truly stationary? Is the sidewalk outside your house stationary? If you're standing on it, you might think of it as motionless—firmly planted on the Earth. But this depends on the frame of reference you're using.

While the sidewalk seems stationary relative to you, the Earth itself is far from still. It's orbiting the Sun at a staggering speed of 67,000 miles per hour. So, to call the sidewalk stationary, we must clarify it is stationary relative to a frame of reference that moves with it. Each object's frame of reference comes with its own set of Cartesian coordinates, and determining whether something is stationary depends on comparing its motion—or lack thereof—relative to another frame.

In summary: the laws of classical physics and the concept of time are absolute within each individual body of reference or position, but they are *relative* in relation to one another. The same fundamental principles of physics apply to both the orbit of the Earth and a "stationary" sidewalk when considered within their own *frames of reference*, but they do not hold true when comparing these frames to each other.

What was Einstein's response to this revelation? He proposed to "drop" the idea of additive velocities and instead approach the problem using the Lorentz Transformation. In his book "Relativity (page 30)" he states, "If we drop these hypothesis, then the dilemma of Section VII *(the incompatibility of additive velocities)* disappears, because the theorem of the addition of velocities derived in Section VI *(additive velocities)* becomes invalid."[52]

Step 2: The Speed of Light is Constant

The second logical step that Einstein took in 1905 was to accept that the speed of light is constant. This constant

---

[52] Italics added for clarity.

speed was first demonstrated by Albert Michelson and Edward Morley in 1887 through the Michelson-Morley experiment.[53]

In their experiment, Michelson and Morley sought to measure the speed of Earth as it moved through a hypothetical medium known as "aether." At the time, many scientists believed that this aether permeated all of space and served as a medium for light waves to propagate. To conduct their measurements, they set up an interferometer, a device that splits a beam of light and then recombines it. This setup was intended to detect any differences in the speed of light depending on the direction of Earth's motion through the aether. The hypothesis was that the speed of light would vary, depending on whether Earth was moving toward or away from the source of light.

However, the results of the Michelson-Morley experiment were unexpected: there was no detectable difference in the speed of light as Earth moved around the Sun at approximately 67,000 miles per hour, regardless of the direction of measurement. This null result was highly significant because it supported the idea that the speed of light is constant in all inertial frames of reference, irrespective of the motion of the source or the observer. Additionally, it raised questions about the concept of additive velocities regarding the speed of light.

Therefore, the second logical step that Einstein took was to accept that the speed of light is constant, which laid the

---

[53] MIT. Lecture 3.3: Michelson-Morley Experiment. Prof. Markus Klute. (Jan. 2021). https://ocw.mit.edu/courses/8-20-introduction-to-special-relativity-january-iap-2021/resources/lecture-3-2/

foundation for his Theory of Special Relativity.

Step 3: The Lorentz Transformation

Although Einstein moved away from the classical concept of additive velocities, he was determined to understand why the theorem did not apply to quantum energy traveling at the speed of light. He achieved this by incorporating Lorentz's transformations into his theory of special relativity, published in 1905.[54] By doing so, he provided a more comprehensive and profound explanation for the constancy of the speed of light.

The Lorentz transformations were introduced by Dutch physicist Hendrik Lorentz in 1895 and were developed in an effort to explain the results of experiments related to the Michelson-Morley experiment, which was discussed in *Step 2*.

In physics, a transformation is an equation that describes how quantities change under different conditions, such as shifts in reference frames, motion, or interactions. A common transformation is the conversion of temperature between Fahrenheit and Celsius.

For example, to convert 68 degrees Fahrenheit to Celsius, you would use the following transformation:

[54] UC Berkeley. Lorentz Transformations in Special Relativity. Robert G. Littlejohn. (Spring 2020). https://bohr.physics.berkeley.edu/classes/221/1112/notes/lorentz.pdf

$$C = 5/9 * (F-32)$$
$$C = 5/9 * (68-32)$$
$$C = 5/9 * 36$$
$$C = 180/9$$
$$C = 20$$

Thus, 20 degrees Celsius is equivalent to 68 degrees Fahrenheit.

Similarly, the Lorentz transformations are a set of equations that explain how measurements of space, time, direction, and quantities such as speed change when shifting from one perspective—or point of observation—to another, particularly when two different reference bodies or Cartesian coordinates are moving independently of each other.

To illustrate the concept of Lorentz transformations, consider the experience of Lewis and Clark during their expedition. Imagine them paddling their canoe on a river. When paddling downstream, the river's current adds to their effort, speeding up their journey. Conversely, when paddling upstream, the current subtracts from their effort, making travel more difficult, or even resulting in no forward movement if their paddling matches the current's speed.

These additive velocities helped them navigate relative to the land around them, just as the Lorentz transformations help us understand how motion and measurements change depending on our observation perspective. Whether observing from the riverbank or from the canoe drifting with the current, these transformations allow us to navigate the "currents" of motion between different viewpoints, revealing how speed and time behave in relative motion.

The Lorentz transformations are essential for understanding relativistic effects, such as time dilation and length contraction. They ensure that the laws of physics, which are universal, and created by God, remain consistent across different inertial frames of reference, as dictated by Einstein's theory of special relativity.

In essence, a transformation in this context refers to the mathematical rules that govern how physical quantities change when *transitioning between different frames of reference.*

While Lorentz originally introduced these transformations to clarify experimental results, it was Einstein who elevated them to fundamental principles within the framework of special relativity as we will see in the next step. The Lorentz transformations remain an essential mathematical tool in modern physics, used to describe the behavior of space and time in relativistic contexts.

Step 4: Every Body of Reference has its Own Time

Imagine being a curious explorer venturing into a hidden cave deep within an ancient forest. Legends say time flows differently within its depths. As you cautiously enter, you navigate twisting tunnels adorned with glistening crystals. Hours seem to pass as you explore, but when you finally emerge, only a few minutes have gone by in the outside world. While this may be fictional, it reflects the real-world phenomenon of *time dilation*, a key concept from Einstein's Theory of Relativity.

In 1905, Einstein made a groundbreaking contribution

by proposing that each frame of reference has its own time, a key concept in his theory of relativity. He describes his "eureka moment" in chapters 8 and 9 of his book *Relativity*, where he examines the idea of *simultaneity*—specifically, the notion that two events can occur at the same time.[55]

Einstein achieved this by a thought experiment involving two lightning strikes. A thought experiment is a mental exercise designed to explore a concept or to analyze the implications of a theory without the need for physical experimentation. It involves imagining a scenario to investigate its consequences, allowing one to consider abstract ideas and their effects in a controlled way.

In this case, the thought experiment involved two simultaneous lightning strikes. Picture the situation: two bolts of lightning strike the ground in different locations at the same time. An observer standing exactly in the middle of both strikes would see the flashes occur simultaneously. However, suppose there's another observer moving towards one of the strikes and away from the other. This observer would perceive the flashes differently, witnessing the lightning from the strike they are approaching first, followed by the other strike, creating the impression that the two events did not occur at the same time.

This scenario illustrates how the perception of time can vary based on an observer's position and motion. Einstein realized this fundamentally challenged the classical idea of an absolute time, demonstrating that time is not universal but instead relative to each observer's frame of reference.

---

[55] Einstein, Albert. Relativity, 15th Edition. Wings Books, New York. June 9, 1952. Pages 30-31

This concept became a cornerstone of the theory of relativity, fundamentally altering our understanding of time and space.

To illustrate this concept, consider GPS satellites. These satellites orbit the Earth at high speeds, and their clocks tick slower when compared to those on the ground.[56]

This difference isn't due to their altitude but to their velocity relative to Earth.

GPS satellites orbit at high speed, so special-relativistic time dilation makes their onboard clocks tick slightly slower than identical clocks on the ground. The net result is that satellite clocks run fast by roughly 38 microseconds per day. Engineers pre-adjust the clocks for this known offset; without the correction, GPS positions would drift by kilometers within a single day.

The *time dilation* observed in GPS satellites is explained by the Lorentz Transformation, a mathematical formula that describes how time and space change between different frames of reference moving at constant velocities relative to one another. Here's how it works:

---

[56] Real-World Relativity: The GPS Navigation System. Pogge, Richard W., Professor, Ohio State University. 3/11/2017. https://www.astronomy.ohio-state.edu/pogge.1/Ast162/Unit5/gps.html

The Equation for Time Dilation

$$\Delta t' = \frac{\Delta t}{\sqrt{1 - \frac{v^2}{c^2}}}$$

Where:

- $\Delta t'$: Time interval in the moving frame.
- Δt: Time interval in the stationary frame.
- v: Relative velocity between the frames.
- c: Speed of light.

Real-World Example: GPS Satellites

Assume a satellite moves at a velocity, $v = 3\times10^7$ m/s (about 10% of the speed of light) relative to Earth, which is just an example, no satellite actually moves that fast. I'm using that velocity to keep the math simple. Then plug in the value for the speed of light, $c = 3\times10^8$ m/s. For a proper time interval $\Delta t = 1$ second, the observed time on Earth, $\Delta t'$, becomes:

$$\Delta t' = \frac{1}{\sqrt{1 - \frac{(3\times10^7)^2}{(3\times10^8)^2}}}$$

Now, calculate:

$$\Delta t' = \frac{1}{\sqrt{1 - 0.01}} = \frac{1}{\sqrt{0.99}} \approx 1.005\ seconds$$

In this hypothetical situation, this tiny adjustment of 1.005 seconds ensures the synchronization of satellite and Earth-based clocks, critical for accurate positioning and ensuring that the map on your smartphone is accurate. And it also demonstrates that time differs based on your frame of reference.

Step 5: The Relationship Between Mass and Energy

Einstein's work on the Lorentz transformation opened the door to a deeper understanding of how space, time, mass, and energy are interconnected. His groundbreaking realization: that mass and energy aren't separate but are two sides of the same coin. This discovery led to the famous equation $E = mc^2$, showing that even an object at rest contains incredible energy locked within its mass.

5a: Momentum - The Power of Motion

Momentum measures the *power* of something in motion. Imagine a bowling ball rolling down a lane. Its momentum—determined by its mass and speed—tells us how hard it is to stop or start it. The faster it rolls or the heavier it is, the more momentum it has. This relationship is captured in the equation:

$$\text{Momentum} = \text{Mass} \times \text{Velocity} \ (\rho = \mu \times \nu)$$

where:

- ρ: The momentum.
- μ: Mass of the object.
- ν: Velocity of the object.

For example, a 2 kg ball rolling at 3 m/s has a momentum of 6 kg·m/s. However, momentum isn't static—it changes as the object's motion and direction shift, just like a basketball flying through the air arcs and twists as it moves.

5b: Adding Time to the Equation (Four-Momentum)

Momentum is traditionally thought of as a single measure: the product of an object's mass and velocity ($\rho = \mu \times \nu$). It describes how hard it is to stop or start something in motion. But Einstein realized this view was incomplete. Momentum isn't just about how fast or heavy something is—it also depends on its direction and the time it takes to move.

Einstein expanded momentum into *four components*, adding time as a dimension to the three spatial directions (x, y, z).[57] This idea, called *four-momentum*, treats momentum as a "package" of information that is represented by an equation.

Each part of the *four-momentum equation* corresponds

---

[57] Einstein, Albert. Relativity, 15th Edition. Wings Books, New York. June 9, 1952. Pages 170-171.

to a specific property:

- $\mu = 0$: Energy divided by the speed of light (E/c).
- $\mu = 1, 2, 3$: Momentum in the x, y, and z directions.

The idea of time is encapsulated in measuring the kinetic energy of mass, which includes velocity, something we are very familiar with. When we drive a car we drive according to the speed limit, or miles per hour. Therefore, the kinetic energy of the car incorporates the concept of time.

By including time, Einstein showed that motion and energy are intertwined in both space and time. This shift in thinking gave us a more complete picture of how objects behave, especially at high speeds, where classical physics starts to break down. Four-momentum unites these ideas into one powerful framework, changing how we understand the universe.

Imagine a basketball player standing on a court. To score a basket, the player must release the ball with the right direction, angle, and force to ensure it arcs through the hoop. As the basketball travels in an arc it is constantly changing direction along the x, y, and z axes. In other words, the momentum is constantly changing as it moves through space.

5c: Solving $E = mc^2$

In classical physics, we calculate an object's kinetic energy using $K = \frac{1}{2}\mu \times v^2$. Velocity is squared because energy doesn't increase linearly with speed—it skyrockets. For example, doubling a car's speed from 30 m/s to 60 m/s quadruples its energy.

But classical physics calculations break down for objects at extremely high speeds. To address this, Einstein developed the energy-momentum relation:

$$E^2 = (pc)^2 + (m_o c^2)^2$$

Terms:

- E: Total energy of the particle.
- p: Relativistic momentum ($p = \gamma mv$).
- c: Speed of light ($\sim 3 \times 10^8$ m/s).
- m_o: Rest mass (mass at rest).
- $(m_o c^2)$: Rest energy (energy from rest mass).

Key Points:

1. $(pc)^2$: Energy from momentum.
2. $(m_o c^2)^2$: Rest energy squared.
3. At rest ($p = 0$): $E = m_o c^2$.
4. For massless particles ($m_o = 0$): $E = pc$.

This equation unifies energy, momentum, and mass in relativity and accounts for both an object's motion (momentum) and its rest energy. *If the object isn't moving, the momentum is zero ($p = 0$)*, and the equation simplifies to the now-famous $E = mc^2$. Even when something is perfectly still, its mass contains enormous energy—a revolutionary idea that redefined physics.

Here is the step-by-step solution:

$$E^2 = (pc)^2 + (m_0c^2)^2$$

$$E^2 = (0 * c)^2 + (m_0c^2)^2$$

$$E^2 = (0)^2 + (m_0c^2)^2$$

$$E^2 = (m_0c^2)^2$$

Simplify the square root:

$$E = mc^2$$

The Architecture of Space and Time

Einstein did not merely address a flaw in classical reasoning.

He changed the way humanity understands time and reality.

When the theorem of additive velocities failed to apply to light, the universe did not descend into contradiction. The failure was not in nature—it was in our assumptions about nature, specifically, the nature of time.

Einstein recognized the *boundary* itself was rooted in the concept of time.

Classical mechanics worked beautifully—but only within limits. Additive velocities applied to boats and rivers, to cannonballs and planets. But they did not apply to light.

Rather than discard order, Einstein refined it.

He adjusted our understanding of space and time so that one fact remained untouched:

The speed of light is constant for every observer, regardless of motion, therefore the concept of time is relative.

That single decision reshaped physics.

To preserve the constancy of light, clocks could no longer be absolute. Distances could no longer be fixed. Simultaneity could no longer be universal. Space and time themselves had to bend—not randomly, but mathematically—so that light would remain constant.

And in doing so, Einstein ushered in a paradigm shift that changed the twentieth century.

Modern physics was born from that recognition.

Nuclear energy. Particle accelerators. GPS navigation. Space exploration. Our understanding of black holes and the expanding universe—all trace back to this moment when Einstein recognized a boundary and refused to ignore it.

But his accomplishment was not merely technical.

It was philosophical.

Humanity had believed that time flowed the same everywhere. That rest was absolute. That motion could always be added like currents in a river.

Einstein showed us that our intuition doesn't always match reality.

He demonstrated that the universe is governed by unchangeable principles that hold even when our common sense fails.

For you and me, this means something profound—it reveals a more precise order.

Einstein began with a flashlight on a moving train. He ended by showing that space and time themselves operate under disciplined laws.

What we discover is an architecture—consistent and astonishingly precise. Architecture that was designed.

The question that now stands before us is unavoidable:

If this is how the universe behaves at extreme velocity, what happens when gravity pushes the boundary of space and time to their breaking point?

Chapter 13: Summary

This chapter explores what happens when motion approaches its ultimate boundary—and how that boundary reshaped our understanding of reality.

For everyday experience, motion follows simple rules. Speeds add together, and time appears constant. But when applied to light, those assumptions break down. No matter how fast the observer moves, the speed of light remains unchanged. What appeared to be a contradiction became the starting point for something deeper.

What Einstein saw—when others did not—was that the problem was not with motion itself, but with time.

Rather than forcing light to fit existing assumptions, he reexamined the foundation. If the speed of light is constant, then time cannot be absolute. It must vary depending on the observer. From that single insight, a new framework emerged—one where space and time are connected, and where motion, energy, and mass are no longer separate ideas, but part of a unified system.

This chapter walks through that reasoning step by step, showing how familiar concepts—like motion, momentum, and reference frames—led to a deeper understanding. Einstein did not discard order; he revealed a more precise one, where even time itself operates within defined limits.

The result was not confusion, but clarity. What seemed like a failure in classical physics became evidence of a deeper structure—one that holds even when intuition does not.

In the end, this chapter shows that the universe does not adjust itself to fit human expectations. It operates according to precise and unchanging principles.

And in uncovering those principles, Einstein revealed something extraordinary:

That even time itself is governed.

14 — Energy-Dominant Singularities

""Ah Lord GOD! Behold, You have made the heavens and the earth by Your great power and by Your outstretched arm! Nothing is too difficult for You."."

Jeremiah 32:17

What happens when velocity and gravity becomes extreme, pushing against the boundaries of physical laws?

Einstein showed that when our assumptions fail, the universe does not fall into contradiction—*it reveals deeper order*. To preserve one invariant—the constancy of light—space and time themselves had to bend.

But special relativity is only the first boundary.

If velocity can force time to dilate and lengths to contract, then gravity can do something even more severe: it can curve spacetime until escape becomes impossible. At that point the question is no longer, *How fast are we moving?* It becomes; *How much reality can be compressed before geometry gives way?*

A black hole is the name we give to that breaking point—where the fabric of spacetime is bent so deeply that even light cannot climb out.

And once we accept Einstein's great equivalence—that *mass and energy are two expressions of the same reality*—we are led to a further question:

If enough mass can collapse spacetime, could enough *energy* do the same?

In general relativity, spacetime does not respond to "mass" in isolation. It responds to energy and momentum. Mass is simply one expression of energy. Einstein's great equivalence ($E = mc^2$) did not merely relate two quantities; it erased the conceptual wall between them. What we call mass is energy in a bound form.

If curvature arises from energy density, then collapse cannot be limited to collapsing stars alone. A star forms a black hole because its energy—expressed as mass—is compressed beyond a critical threshold. But energy itself carries the same gravitational authority.

The question, then, is unavoidable: if sufficient energy can be confined within a small enough volume, would spacetime respond in the same way?

This chapter explores that threshold—not merely a star collapsing into darkness, but the possibility of collapse driven by concentrated energy itself: an *Energy-Dominant Singularity*.

What follows is a thought experiment—a speculative

extension of general relativity and $E=mc^2$. Speculation is the birthplace of new ideas, research and experimentation.

While classical physics permits energy to curve spacetime, quantum field theory raises some questions because we are unable to fully understand what happens at these extremes. That mystery is what makes the adventure of studying the created universe to intriguing.

What is an Energy-Dominant Singularity?

Traditionally, black holes are thought to form when a star collapses in on itself.[58] However, when examining black holes from the perspective of quantum energy, it is quite possible that black holes can form not only from mass but also from concentrated energy alone.

That's why I propose a new hypothetical construct (or thought experiment), an Energy-Dominant Singularity (EDS)—a black hole driven entirely by energy. This challenges the traditional understanding of black hole formation and offers a fresh perspective on the intricate design of the universe.

Warping Spacetime: The Shockwave of Photon Collapse

In a sonic boom, a jet moving faster than the speed of sound compresses air in front of it, where waves collapse upon themselves, creating a shock wave of highly concentrated energy. To understand photon collapse using

---

[58] Lerner, Louise. "*Black holes, explained.*" Univ. of Chicago. https://news.uchicago.edu/explainer/black-holes-explained

this analogy, let's start with the photon's energy:

$$\mathbf{E = hf}$$

Using Einstein's equation:

$$\mathbf{m = E / c^2 = hf / c^2}$$

Therefore, as the frequency (**f**) of a photon increases, its equivalent mass $\mathbf{m = hf / c^2}$ increases. This represents the photon's relativistic mass equivalent. As **f** increases, this equivalent mass grows, leading to stronger gravitational effects despite the photon being massless in the classical sense.

At some critical point, the **energy density = hf / V** becomes so extreme that the wavefront (analogous to the photon's spatial extent) collapses. This collapse generates a **spacetime shockwave**, analogous to the air compression in a sonic boom. It is not merely a smooth scaling of volume but involves dynamic, nonlinear interactions where spacetime curvature increases explosively.

Photon Collapse to a Black Hole

Intense electromagnetic fields can increase a photon's energy density, potentially leading to collapse. The Zeeman Effect, previously discussed, shows how electromagnetic fields can raise a photon's frequency. Picture a gamma-ray photon passing through a collapsing star.[59] The intense electromagnetic fields act like a coiled spring, compressing

---

[59] NASA. Francis Reddy. *What Are Black Holes?* (Sept. 8, 2020). https://www.nasa.gov/universe/what-are-black-holes/

the photon's wavelength and increasing its energy density.

As the gamma-ray compresses (figure 12.1), the angle θ decreases, approaching zero. This intensifies the energy density by decreasing the volume, setting the stage for what can be termed **photon collapse**.

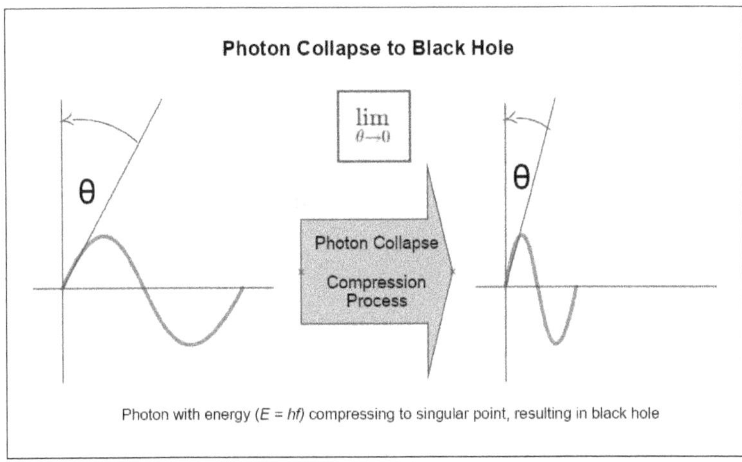

Figure 12.1: Photon Collapse to a Black Hole

The Zeeman Effect and related phenomena can shorten its wavelength, effectively 'compressing' the wavefront. The angle θ in our simplified visualization approaches zero but never quite reaches it in any finite process.

As this compression intensifies, classical intuition suggests the energy density could rise dramatically. We have no complete description of what happens in that ultra-extreme regime—quantum gravity remains beyond our reach.

Yet this very frontier invites the question: if energy density were to climb without the dissipation mechanisms we currently understand, could spacetime respond with runaway curvature? This is the conceptual heart of the Energy-Dominant Singularity.

The Energy-Dominant Singularity

Photons undergoing constructive interference may be able to create energy densities capable of collapsing spacetime. When waves align—peak to peak and trough to trough—their combined energy forms a much more powerful wave. This phenomenon is similar to a sonic boom when a supersonic jet causes sound waves to merge into a shockwave.

If energy can bend spacetime in small amounts, what happens when it's confined and concentrated in extreme conditions? The answer lies in the formation of an *Energy-Dominant Singularity (EDS)* (figure 12.2), where energy, rather than mass, drives black hole formation.

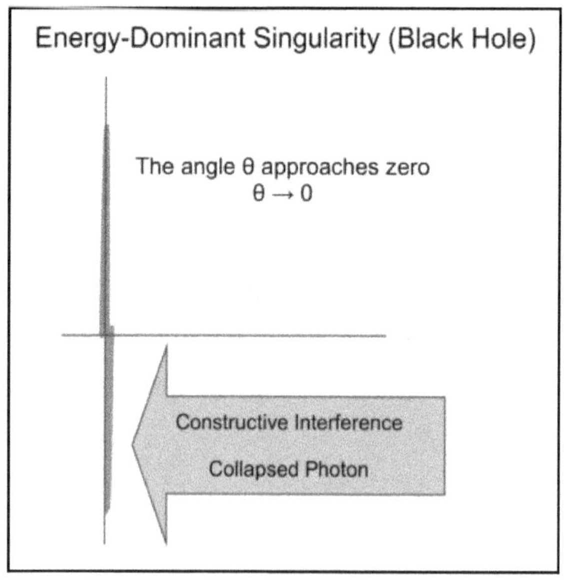

Figure 12.2: The Energy-Dominant Singularity

How to Turn the Earth into a Black Hole

Imagine holding a tiny marble about 9 millimeters wide.[60] What if someone told you it had the mass of the entire Earth? It sounds absurd—but it illustrates a powerful concept.

The **Schwarzschild radius** refers to the size something must be compressed to for its gravity to become so strong that not even light can escape. This "event horizon" marks the boundary of a black hole.

The formula for a black hole of this nature is:

$$\mathbf{r_s = 2GM / c^2}$$

Where:

- G = gravitational constant
- M = relativistic mass
- c = speed of light

Squeezing Earth's mass into a 9 mm ball would create a black hole.

Now let's go further. What if, instead of mass, we considered light itself? Light has no rest mass but carries energy, and thanks to $E = mc^2$, energy and mass are equivalent. Light's energy can also be expressed as:

[60] 9mm = 0.35 inches, or approx. ⅜".

$$\mathbf{E = hf}$$

Where h is Planck's constant and f is the frequency. Substituting into the Schwarzschild formula:

$$\mathbf{r_s = 2G(hf / c^2) / c^2}$$

Simplify by multiplying numerator and denominator by c^2:

$$\mathbf{r_s = 2Ghf / c^4}$$

This equation reveals something important: **Energy can mimic mass**. When energy is confined to a space smaller than its Schwarzschild radius, spacetime collapses into a black hole.[61] Even light can bend spacetime when packed tightly enough.

Thus, the Schwarzschild radius tells us that once energy density crosses a critical threshold, it forms a black hole, or as proposed here, an Energy-Dominant Singularity (EDS).

How Light Tears a Hole in Spacetime

Imagine compressing a spring. As the volume shrinks, energy is packed into a smaller space. Compress the spring fully, and the windings touch. If the spring were a wave, it would collapse on itself and release a shockwave—like a sonic boom.

---

[61] Anderson, James L. (2001). "V.C The Schwarzschild Field, Event Horizons, and Black Holes". In Meyer, Robert A. (ed.). Encyclopedia of Physical Science and Technology (Third Edition). Cambridge, Massachusetts: Academic Press. ISBN 978-0-12-227410-7. Retrieved 23 October 2023.

This illustrates **energy density**:

$$\text{Energy Density} = \text{Energy} / \text{Volume}$$

Photons—tiny particles of light—gain energy with higher frequency:

$$E = hf$$

As energy rises, the Schwarzschild radius shrinks:

$$rs = 2Ghf / c^4$$

And its volume:

$$V = 4/3\pi(rs^3) = 4/3\pi(2Ghf / c^4)^3$$

Simplifies to:

$$V = (32G^3h^3f^3) / (3c^{12})$$

This tiny volume determines whether a gamma-ray photon can produce an EDS. Using real constants, the volume of a collapsed gamma-ray becomes:

$$V \approx 5.45392 \times 10^{-165} \text{ m}^3$$

That's 10^{135} times smaller than a hydrogen atom or 10^{155} times *smaller than a grain of sand.*

The Energy Density of an EDS

Now calculate the energy density of a collapsing photon:[62]

---

[62] George B. Arfken, Hans J. Weber, and Frank E. Harris, Mathematical Methods for Physicists (Elsevier, 2013).

$$\rho = hf / V$$

Substituting for V:

$$\rho = hf / [(32G^3h^3f^3) / (3c^{12})] = (3c^{12}) / (32G^3h^2f^2)$$

Although f^2 appears in the denominator, as f increases, V decreases even faster—causing ρ to grow exponentially. As $V \to 0, \rho \to \infty$.

This extreme energy concentration bends spacetime to the point of collapse, forming a black hole. Though massless, photons can warp spacetime when energy density reaches critical levels.

Think of the spring again: the tighter it's compressed, the more concentrated its energy. When fully compressed, it doesn't disappear—it becomes an unstoppable force. For photons, that force is their *energy density,* collapsing spacetime into an *EDS.*

Nonlinear Energy Density

Nonlinear energy density occurs when energy becomes so concentrated it distorts spacetime, leading to phenomena like black holes. It mirrors the boundless nature of God's power.

In a nuclear reactor meltdown, energy density can rise from 10^6 W/m³ to 10^8 W/m³ or more. A similar runaway process occurs during photon collapse.

This can be compared to God's overwhelming presence—*"You cannot see My face, for no man can see Me and live"* (Exodus 33:20). Just as black holes defy comprehension, God's infinite power transcends understanding.

A helpful analogy: imagine a trampoline with a heavy ball. As the weight increases, the dip deepens, pulling more fabric in.[63] This illustrates nonlinear energy: as more energy is packed in, the spacetime "fabric" pulls harder in response.

Nonlinear Collapse Equation

Consider the photon's energy density near collapse:

$$\rho = (hf / V)(1 + hf / c^4)$$

- hf / V: basic energy density
- $1 + hf / c^4$: nonlinear correction term
- As hf increases, the nonlinear term amplifies ρ, accelerating the collapse.[64]

When energy density becomes nonlinear, the feedback loop between energy and curvature drives collapse to extreme levels.[65] The photon becomes so dense it triggers a **spacetime singularity**.[66]

A Practical Analogy

Think of a snowball rolling downhill. Initially slow, it gains mass and momentum, becoming unstoppable.

---

63 V. Petrosian, "Nonlinear Effects in High-Energy Astrophysics," Astrophysical Journal 248 (1981): 303-311.

64 Banesh Hoffmann, "Nonlinear Electrodynamics: Singularities and Black Holes," Physical Review 47, no. 10 (1935): 877-890.

65 J. Robert Oppenheimer and Hartland Snyder, "On Continued Gravitational Contraction," Physical Review 56, no. 5 (1939): 455-459.

66 George B. Arfken, Hans J. Weber, and Frank E. Harris, Mathematical Methods for Physicists (Elsevier, 2013).

Nonlinear energy density is like that snowball—self-reinforcing and accelerating collapse.

Critical Condition: Infinite Energy Density

As the frequency increases toward infinity $f \to \infty$ and $V \to 0$, the nonlinear term dominates. The result is:

- A **spacetime shockwave**, where geometry is torn apart.
- A point of nearly infinite density and curvature: the Energy-Dominant Singularity.

The photon, compressed by effects like the Zeeman Effect, becomes infinitely dense. Constructive interference then releases a shockwave, forming an EDS.

The Energy-Dominant Black Hole Equation

At extremely small scales, where **energy alone** dominates spacetime curvature, the mass term in $\mathbf{E = mc^2}$ becomes negligible. Instead, energy and volume define the relationship:

$$E = c^2V$$

As $\mathbf{V} \to 0$ and $\mathbf{E} \to \infty$, we arrive at the expression for an energy-dominant singularity:

$$E = c^2$$

The Constancy of Light as a Reflection of God's Nature

When Einstein discovered that light would not obey

additive velocities, reality did not unravel—it tightened. Space and time adjusted so that one invariant would remain unbroken.

But an Energy-Dominant Singularity forces the question of cosmic boundaries even deeper.

Here, the issue is not whether time can stretch or clocks can disagree. The issue is whether spacetime itself can survive unlimited concentration. Whether geometry has a boundary. Whether creation contains a built-in "no farther."

And it does.

The Schwarzschild radius is not just a formula. It is a line etched into the architecture of reality—a boundary: *compress beyond this threshold, and escape ends*. Light does not slow. Physics does not become sloppy. The universe does not improvise. It obeys.

That is the sobering thought: even at the edge of infinity, the constants do not wobble. The numbers that govern light and gravity remain steady while everything else gives way.

And for you and me, that matters.

Because we live in a world that often feels unstable—where institutions shake, bodies weaken, and plans fail—yet the deeper lesson of the universe is this: ultimate reality is not held together by human effort. It is sustained by law, by coherence, by boundaries that do not apologize. The question is: who established these laws and boundaries?

If creation remains ordered even where spacetime tears, then order is not an accident.

It is governance.

It is design.

And the God who set the limits of light and the thresholds of collapse is not threatened by the extremes He built into His own creation. The singularity is not a place where God disappears. It is a place where human intuition fails—and where the depth of His architecture becomes undeniable.

So we end where Einstein began, with a boundary.

Not merely the constancy of light, but the constancy of the One who authored the laws light obeys.

Energy-Dominant Singularities

Einstein showed us something surprising. When objects move near the speed of light, clocks do not keep normal time, and rulers do not keep normal length. Time slows. Length contracts. But one thing does not change: the speed of light remains the same.

Instead of the universe breaking down under extreme motion, space and time adjust to protect that constant. The measurements shift. The structure holds.

That was the first boundary.

If velocity can bend time, gravity can bend spacetime. If mass can collapse geometry, energy must carry the same authority. And if energy density rises without restraint, then collapse is not limited to dying stars. It becomes a question of concentration.

We followed that logic to its threshold.

A photon has no rest mass, but it carries energy.
Energy is equivalent to mass.
Mass curves spacetime.
Therefore, energy density curves spacetime.

As frequency rises, equivalent mass rises.
As volume shrinks, density explodes.
As density increases, curvature accelerates.

The mathematics does not drift into chaos. It intensifies toward a boundary.

The Schwarzschild radius marks that boundary. Compress beyond it, and the ability to escape ends. Whether we squeeze the Earth into a 9-millimeter sphere or confine electromagnetic energy within an infinitesimal volume, the same architectural law applies.

Energy, when concentrated, can mimic mass.
Energy, when confined, can dominate curvature.

This is the conceptual horizon of the Energy-Dominant Singularity.

We examined photon collapse, constructive interference, nonlinear amplification, and runaway curvature.

Each step revealed the same pattern: as energy density approaches infinity, geometry approaches its limit. Not gradually. Not casually. But through accelerating feedback—like a snowball, like a sonic boom, like a trampoline pulled beyond tolerance.

And yet something remarkable remains.

Even at infinite density, the constants hold.
The speed of light remains fixed.
The gravitational constant does not hesitate.
The equations do not improvise.

The universe does not become disordered at its extremes. It becomes more exact.

That is the deeper revelation of this chapter.

A singularity is not evidence of chaos.
It is evidence of boundary.

It is a "no farther" written into the fabric of existence.

If energy can be compressed to the edge of collapse and still obey law, then reality is not sustained by accident. It is governed. It is structured. It is authored.

The Energy-Dominant Singularity is not merely a thought experiment about black holes. It is a lens through which we see that even where spacetime tears, order remains sovereign.

And that brings us back to where Einstein began—with an invariant—the speed of light remains unchanged.

Not only the constancy of light, but the constancy of the One who established the limits light cannot cross.

Chapter 14: Summary

This chapter pushes the limits of what we have seen so far and asks: *what happens when energy and gravity reach their extreme?*

Einstein showed that when motion approaches the speed of light, space and time adjust to preserve a constant. But when gravity becomes extreme, spacetime itself begins to bend—and eventually, collapse. A black hole marks that boundary, where escape is no longer possible.

This chapter takes that idea one step further. If mass and energy are equivalent, then collapse is not limited to matter alone. Under the right conditions, energy itself can be concentrated to the point where it dominates spacetime curvature. This leads to the concept of an *Energy-Dominant Singularity*—a theoretical point where energy density becomes so extreme that it produces the same effect as a collapsing star.

Through examples like photon compression, constructive interference, and increasing energy density, the chapter shows how this collapse could occur. As energy is confined into smaller volumes, its effects do not diminish—they intensify. What begins as measurable interaction accelerates toward a boundary where spacetime can no longer sustain itself in its normal form.

Yet even at that edge, something remains unchanged. The constants do not break. The laws do not weaken. As conditions become more extreme, the structure of reality does not dissolve—it becomes more exact.

In the end, this chapter reveals that *a singularity is not a sign of chaos, but of boundary.* It marks a limit built into creation itself—a point where nothing further can be compressed or escaped.

And that boundary points to something deeper:

A universe that holds together—even at its most extreme—is not sustained by accident.

It is governed.

15 — Time Dilation

"For My thoughts are not your thoughts, Nor are your ways My ways," declares the Lord. "For as the heavens are higher than the earth, So are My ways higher than your ways And My thoughts than your thoughts."

Isaiah 55:8-9

You live by time.

You rise by it. You schedule by it. You measure your successes and your failures by it. Every plan you make assumes that tomorrow will arrive in the same steady rhythm as today.

But near a black hole, that rhythm falters.

Imagine drifting toward the event horizon. Your watch ticks. Your thoughts feel clear. You reach forward—and from your perspective nothing is unusual. Yet to an observer far away, your movement slows. Your gestures stretch. The final moments before crossing the horizon seem to lengthen without end.

From their vantage point, you never quite arrive.

Time does not shatter.

It elongates.

It seems to freeze.

And when time itself begins to stretch toward infinity, physics exposes something profound: the universe is not bound to the clock in your hand.

Gravitational Time Dilation at the Event Horizon

The infinite stretching of time near a black hole's event horizon through gravitational time dilation serves as a metaphor for God's transcendence over time and His existence beyond temporal constraints.

Time moves slower in stronger gravitational fields.[67] If you were near the event horizon of a black hole, time would pass more slowly for you than for someone farther away. This happens because gravity warps space and time, making clocks (and everything else) run slower. It's as if gravity is stretching time itself.

Near the event horizon, the time dilation experienced at a distance *r* from the black hole is represented by:

$$\Delta t' = \Delta t \sqrt{1 - \frac{r_s}{r}}$$

[67] Einstein, A. (February 2004). Relativity : the Special and General Theory by Albert Einstein.

Where:

- $\Delta t'$ is the time interval experienced by an observer at radius r,
- Δt is the time interval measured far from the object (in a stationary reference frame),
- r_s is the Schwarzschild radius.

As r (your distance from the event horizon) approaches r_s, the **event horizon**, the term **($1 - r_s / r$)** approaches zero, causing the **time interval** experienced by the observer $\boldsymbol{\Delta t'}$ to approach **infinity**. To a distant observer, time appears to "freeze" at the event horizon.

This stretching of time toward infinity due to **gravitational time dilation** near the event horizon demonstrates the profound influence of energy density and spacetime curvature.

When we observe a black hole, we are witnessing the most extreme distortion of time and space in the known universe. Near the event horizon, time stretches toward infinity, revealing how profoundly energy and gravity can shape spacetime itself.

The universe itself is built upon quantum energy—the foundational substance from which all matter emerges. Yet even this foundation exists within time and space. God, however, existed before the universe began. He is not bound by time but transcends it completely.

Black holes therefore provide a remarkable glimpse of the limits of our universe. At these boundaries of physics—

where time stretches toward infinity—we are reminded that the Creator of the universe exists beyond time itself.

Lorentz Transformation for Time Dilation

Einstein recognized that time was the key to relativity. Time dilation of an **energy-dependent singularity (EDS)** can also be expressed in terms of Einstein's Special Relativity $E = mc^2$ and the Lorentz Transformation.[68] The formula for relativistic time dilation is:

$$\Delta t' = \frac{\Delta t}{\sqrt{1 - \frac{v^2}{c^2}}}$$

Recall our discussion on inertial frames of reference: a GPS satellite and the Earth move at constant velocities relative to each other. Now, imagine sitting in the middle of the quantum raindrop. You would experience two frames of reference moving at constant velocities relative to one another: the linear vector moving at the speed of light, and the circular vector (representing the frequency) moving at less than the speed of light. But what happens when the circular vector approaches the speed of light?

---

68 Rao, K. N. Srinivasa (1988). The Rotation and Lorentz Groups and Their Representations for Physicists (illustrated ed.). John Wiley & Sons. p. 213.

If the circular velocity of the quantum "raindrop" approaches the speed of light (3 x 10^8 meters per second), and we apply the Lorentz transformation time dilation equation, we can calculate the time dilation factor. So, let's start with:

$$\Delta t' = \frac{\Delta t}{\sqrt{1 - \frac{v^2}{c^2}}}$$

Step 1: Substitute $v \to c$.

Let's plug in the values when the circular vector approaches the speed of light.

- $v = 3 \times 10^8$ meters per second (approaches the speed of light).
- $c = 3 \times 10^8$ meters per second.

$$\Delta t' = \frac{\Delta t}{\sqrt{1 - \frac{(300{,}000{,}000)^2}{(3 \times 10^8)^2}}}$$

$$\Delta t' = \frac{\Delta t}{\sqrt{1 - \frac{90{,}000{,}000{,}000{,}000{,}000}{90{,}000{,}000{,}000{,}000{,}000}}}$$

As the circular vector approaches the speed of light $v \to c$, the term $v^2 / c^2 \to 1$:

$$\Delta t' = \frac{\Delta t}{\sqrt{1 - \frac{1}{1}}}$$

Step 2: Simplify the denominator:

$$\sqrt{1-1} = \sqrt{0} = 0$$

This leads to:

$$\Delta t' = \frac{\Delta t}{0}$$

Step 3: Interpret the result:

Dividing by zero implies the time difference tends toward infinity, not reaching it but approaching it:

$$\Delta t' \rightarrow \infty$$

Energy-Dominant Singularity

When we combine gravitational time dilation with the Lorentz transformation, a striking pattern emerges. Whether through velocity approaching the speed of light or gravity approaching the event horizon, the result is the same: **time stretches toward infinity**.

Different paths. Same boundary.

As **velocity** approaches *c*, the denominator in the Lorentz equation approaches zero, and the time interval grows without bound.

As **radius** approaches the Schwarzschild limit, gravitational time dilation intensifies until motion appears to slow without limit.

In both cases, the universe signals that we are nearing a threshold.

Time does not simply run faster or slower—it approaches suspension.

This is not coincidence. It is architecture.

In Chapter 14 we explored the possibility that extreme energy density can collapse spacetime into an Energy-Dominant Singularity. Now we see what such a collapse implies for time itself. As energy concentrates and curvature intensifies, time ceases to behave in familiar ways. It stretches. It elongates. It resists completion.

And this touches something deeply personal.

We live inside time. We measure our lives by it. We fear losing it. We try to control it.

Yet the universe quietly reveals that time is not ultimate. It bends under sufficient energy. It slows under sufficient gravity. It approaches infinity at defined physical boundaries.

If time can be stretched within creation, then it is not the highest reality.

It is governed.

Isaiah reminds us that God's ways are higher than ours. Physics gives us a glimpse of what that means. At the edge of a black hole, time approaches stillness—not because it fails, but because it is subject to deeper laws.

The One who authored spacetime is not contained within it.

Gravitational time dilation does not prove God's eternity. But it reveals something consistent with it: creation itself contains boundaries where time loses its authority.

And at that boundary, we are reminded—Our clocks measure duration.

But God measures eternity.

When Time Bends

You organize your life by time.

You wake to it.
You measure your days by it.
You look back on it and wonder where it went.

Time governs every human life.

Yet the universe quietly tells us that time is not the final authority.

Near a black hole, time stretches.

A second becomes longer.
Moments refuse to complete.
From a distance, motion freezes at the event horizon.

Physics does not say time breaks.

It says time bends.

Whether through velocity approaching the speed of light or gravity approaching the event horizon, the message is the same. The equations change. The path is different. But the boundary is identical.

Time stretches toward infinity.

That discovery reveals something profound.

Time is not the foundation of reality.

It is part of creation—it was created in the same moment light was created.

And anything that is part of creation must itself have a Creator.

The universe contains places where time slows almost to stillness. But God is not slowed. He does not wait for tomorrow. He does not move from past to future.

He simply **is**.

The God who spoke light into existence is not governed by the clock that governs us. He stands outside the fabric of spacetime itself.

When we study the deepest structures of the universe—energy, motion, gravity, and singularities—we are not merely studying physics.

We are glimpsing the architecture of a creation that points beyond itself.

Our clocks measure seconds.

Our calendars measure years.

But the Creator of the universe measures eternity.

And the closer we look at the universe He made, the

clearer that truth becomes.

Chapter 15: Summary

This chapter turns to something we all live by but rarely question—time.

In everyday life, time feels steady and reliable. We plan by it, measure by it, and assume it moves the same everywhere. But at the edges of the universe, that assumption breaks down. Near a black hole, time does not stop—it stretches, and motion slows as it approaches the event horizon.

Einstein showed that time is not absolute. It changes with motion. When gravity becomes extreme, time bends further, stretching toward infinity. Whether through velocity near the speed of light or gravity near a singularity, time responds to deeper laws.

This chapter shows that *time is not the foundation of reality*. It is part of creation, shaped by the same forces that govern energy and motion.

If time can bend within creation, then it is not ultimate. It is governed.

And if time is governed, then the One who created it is not bound by it.

In the end, this chapter reveals a truth that reaches beyond physics:

We live within time.
But God is not bound by it—He transcends it.

16 — Black Holes and Eternity

"He is before all things, and in Him all things hold together."

Colossians 1:17

We have journeyed to the outer edges of the universe — from the first flash of light in Genesis to the building blocks of energy, from the elegant mathematics of relativity to the silent, relentless power of black holes.

At every step, the same pattern has emerged: the deeper we look into creation, the more we discover order instead of chaos, boundaries instead of anarchy, and coherence instead of accident.

Now we stand at the final threshold.

Black holes represent the most extreme structures in the physical universe. Near their event horizons, gravity becomes so intense that light itself cannot escape. Time stretches toward infinity.

To a distant observer, anything approaching the horizon appears to slow, freeze, and never quite cross over. What we witness is not a breakdown of reality, but its outermost limit—a place where the familiar rules of space and time bend under the weight of creation's own laws.

Yet even here, at the brink of what physics can describe, the universe does not descend into disorder. The constants hold. The equations remain precise. The speed of light, the gravitational relationships, the mathematical boundaries—all continue to obey the same intelligible governance we have seen from quantum scales to galactic structures.

Black holes do not prove the universe is random. They reveal how profoundly ordered it is, even where human intuition fails.

This order points beyond the physical.

Time feels absolute to us. We rise by it, measure our days by it, and often feel crushed beneath its pressure. We fear running out of it. We try desperately to control it. But near a black hole, time is not ultimate. It bends under gravity. It stretches under velocity. It approaches suspension at defined boundaries. Anything that can be stretched or governed is not the highest reality. It is part of creation—and anything created must have a Creator.

The God who spoke "Let there be light" is not bound by the fabric of spacetime He brought into existence. He does not move from past to future as we do. He simply is. Before the mountains were born or the universe expanded from its first moment, He existed — "from everlasting to everlasting" (Psalm 90:2). He stands outside the limits that confine us, yet He sustains every law that governs galaxies and black holes alike. "He is before all things, and in Him all things hold together" (Colossians 1:17).This is where physics reaches its edge and Scripture carries us further.

The same God whose power is displayed in the bending of time and the curving of space entered our time-bound world in the person of Jesus Christ. Eternity stepped into history. Light entered darkness. He lived within the very limits we experience—hunger, weariness, suffering, and death itself—yet He was not mastered by them.

Unlike a black hole, where light cannot escape, the resurrection declares that light cannot be contained. Death did not hold Him. The tomb could not confine the One who authored life. In that singular event, the convergence of eternity and time became visible: the Creator who set the boundaries of the universe conquered the ultimate boundary of death.

This is the true singularity—not the collapse of spacetime, but the moment when infinite love intersected finite history.

And here is what it means for you.

You do not have to live as if time is your ultimate master or uncertainty your constant companion. The God who governs black holes and holds the universe together offers to hold your life as well. When you recognize Him as Creator and King—when you see His fingerprints in the ordered cosmos and respond to His invitation through Christ —

everything changes.

Your identity is no longer something you must frantically construct or defend. It is given by the One who made you in His image.

Your purpose is no longer negotiable or elusive. It is discovered in alignment with the King whose kingdom will ultimately prevail.

Your security is no longer fragile, dependent on shifting circumstances or your own strength. It rests in the unchanging character of the God who sustains the constants of physics and the promises of Scripture.

Pressure and uncertainty will still come. Time will still pass. But they no longer define you. You are anchored in something—Someone—greater than the limits of creation.

The universe is not silent. It declares the eternal power and divine nature of its Author (Romans 1:20). Black holes, far from undermining faith, serve as powerful reminders: even at the extremes of reality, order prevails because a wise and sovereign God prevails.

The same God who set the unbreakable speed of light and allowed time to dilate near a black hole offers you something no physical law can provide—forgiveness for your failures, restoration for what rebellion fractured, and eternal life beyond the reach of any event horizon.

He invites you not merely to admire the cosmos from a distance, but to know its Creator personally. Not to master the mysteries of the universe, but to be reconciled to the One who holds it all together.

When you truly see Him — through the majesty of black holes or the mercy of the cross — your view of reality, of yourself, and of your future cannot remain the same.

Everything changes.

And in that change, you finally find the deep security, clarity, and peace your heart has been longing for.

Chapter 16: Summary

This chapter brings the journey to its final question: *what do the most extreme structures in the universe reveal about the One who created them?*

From light and energy to motion, boundaries, and black holes, the same pattern has emerged—order, precision, and limits that do not fail. Even at the edge of a black hole, where time stretches and light cannot escape, the universe does not descend into chaos. It remains governed.

That boundary reveals something deeper. Time, which feels absolute to us, is not ultimate. It bends, stretches, and approaches its limit under the laws of creation. And anything that can be governed is not the highest reality—it is part of what was created.

This chapter then turns to what physics alone cannot answer. The God who established these laws is not contained within them. He exists beyond time, yet He entered it. In Jesus Christ, eternity stepped into history. And unlike a black hole, where light cannot escape, the resurrection declares that light cannot be contained.

That is the true turning point—not in theory, but in reality.

It is no longer simply a matter of what the universe reveals, but how you will respond to what has been revealed. You are not outside this system. You are part of it—created with purpose, not by accident.

In the end, this chapter makes clear that the message of

creation is not distant or abstract. It is personal.

The God who holds the universe together invites you to know Him.

And when you truly see Him—everything changes.

About the Author

Mike Grayson is convinced that the universe is shouting the glory of its Creator—from the silent majesty of black holes and the intricate dance of quantum energy to the breathtaking expanse of the night sky, the miracle of a newborn child's first spark of life, the towering mountains, and the boundless ocean. All of it reveals the transcendent God who spoke light into existence and sustains every law that governs reality.

For decades Mike worked in engineering, advanced communications systems, and cybersecurity, immersed in the complex order of the physical world. At the same time, he earned a master's degree at Dallas Theological Seminary, diving deeply into the Scriptures that describe the Author behind that order. The longer he studied both, the clearer it became: *science and Scripture are not rivals but complementary witnesses to the same sovereign God.*

Black Holes and Other Works of God was born from this lifelong conviction—that when we truly see God in the grandeur of His creation, everything changes. Mike's passion is to help readers encounter the living Creator whose power is displayed in the stars and whose intimate care is revealed in every human life, inviting all to know Him personally through Jesus Christ.

Mike lives in Texas with his wife, Pam. They are blessed with four children and nine grandchildren.

Main Index

H

I

U

W

Z

Scripture Index

Psalms

Proverbs

Ecclesiastes

Isaiah

Jeremiah

Ezekiel

Matthew

Mark

Luke

John

Acts

Romans

---

1 Corinthians

---

2 Corinthians

Galatians

Ephesians

Philippians

Colossians

---

2 Timothy

Hebrews

---

1 John

Revelation

Name Index

J

K

L

M

www.ingramcontent.com/pod-product-compliance
Lightning Source LLC
LaVergne TN
LVHW012339100826
845148LV00018B/2844

* 9 7 8 0 9 8 1 7 7 7 5 5 9 *